Dallying in Nepal

A Trek in the Sun

What others are saying about Dallying In Nepal....

"I have just finished the last paragraph of Dallying In Nepal – exhausted, enchanted, and thoroughly happy ...... joyful that the author was obviously very in-tune with his journey. I loved it."

Linda Komornik
Corporate Director of Sales & Marketing
Great American Hotel Group

"Dormire is certainly one who doesn't skimp on adventure. Having embarked on a solo vacation to Nepal, he enlightens us with his poignant observations from Kathmandu to the awe-inspiring vistas of the Himalayan Mountains. I enjoyed reading Dallying In Nepal. Great Book!"

Alan Aronoff
CEO, U.S. Information Search,
Diet & Health Coach,Author of Diet Success Strategies

"In October 2012, Byron Dormire took a trip to Nepal, in part to cross off the item on his 'bucket list', but more to experience the vast Himalayan Mountains for himself. Once there, he grasped a sense of the spiritual influences that so dominate that region of the world. His short journey covered some 7 days and he packs a lot into this nicely structured book.

Recommended, particularly if you're looking to add to your own "bucket list" of adventure. I enjoyed it very much."

Peter .J. Williams, *Colonel (CAN) (OF-5)*
Senior Coalition Force Officer at KMTC
Camp ALAMO Kabul, Afghanistan.

Dallying in Nepal

A Trek in the Sun

by

B. T. Dormire

Copyright © 2012 by Byron T. Dormire

Blue Sun Productions, Inc.
7950 Vectra Drive
Colorado Springs, Colorado 80920
Skyrunner77@hotmail.com

Everest Trekking Route Map
Used by permission from Ganga Raj Thapa and The Nepal Hiking Team.
Copyright © Nepal Hiking Team, Ltd.
www.nepalhikingteam.com

Book & Cover Design; John and Dane Low, EbookLaunch.com

Author Photo – Logan Mahone

Everest Region Trekking Destinations

Map courtesy of The Nepal Hiking Team at
www.nepalhikingteam.com

Table of Contents

☯

Part I: The Journey to Namche Bazar

I stopped halfway up the first mile-long rock-strewn stair case. I asked a Sherpa carrying an 80-kilo load trudging up the path, *"Namche, na jik cha?* (Is Namche close by?)"

He looked at me with reverence in his eyes and said, "Na jik *cha,* (It is nearby.)"

My pitiful aches had me whining from toe to eyebrow with all of my fifteen pound sundry trail pack. My guide was way ahead and I'd already lost sight of my porter. "How far is it again?" I asked once more.

He looked at me this time as if I needed 'special help', but smiled anyway, knowing I'd survive despite my inclination to whimper as Americans often did these days. "For men like us...," he said to me in measured English, "it is still *very* far." And he politely motioned for me to slog on ahead.

☯

The Tibet Guest House - Prelude to Lukla

Day 1 - 7 October, 2012

Nepal: I had finally arrived.

We approached the dawn landing at the Tribhuvan International Airport in Kathmandu and I was awakened by a series of small, turbulent jolts. Orange, piercing sunbeams shown obliquely through the aircraft's port side windows and I felt a new degree of excitement as I stretched over and around other passengers to catch a glimpse of what was waiting outside.

Still thousands of feet to go in our descent, I caught only a fair view of the Himalayas off in the distance. Their jagged, razor sharp peaks climbed high above the lower mountain base and winding river valleys. I wondered if one of them wasn't the pinnacle I was looking for in my quest, the tallest triumph yet to add to my bucket list. Were the earthly ramparts of this strange and beautiful land ready to become part of my collected destiny? Would I finally get to hike near Mount Everest and gaze at it in awe, feeling as if it required something else of me besides blubbering in front of it in witlessness?

For years I've imagined making this trip to Nepal for a couple of reasons. First, I saw the fierce, snow-capped backdrop daring me to try and conquer its heights. I wondered if I'd be welcomed there, posing as a worldly man, following the paths of legends. And second, as our jet descended low over the golden roofed temples of the capital city, could I blend into the spiritual realm of this country and not be scolded by the gods for even thinking such a thing? I pondered this second thought and asked which fate for me they'd prefer - being gored off a span bridge by a stampeding Yak, *my personal choice*, or getting run over in the temple hill district by some bus that just lost its brakes?

It was still early outside, and my chances of survival so far looked pretty good. Maybe after 7:00 a.m. and being cleared out of airport customs things would be different. For now, however, the sun's light cast a soothing spell through the layered, blackish mist, that blanket of thick charcoal colored smog that envelops Kathmandu, twenty-four/seven. Air pollution, I was told, always drifted in from India and Pakistan from the south.

"It's killing our glaciers," my guide, Hansah, would later explain. Nepal's rugged peaks soared above this layer and claimed a five-hundred-mile stretch of earth no soot could ever touch. The mountains up there are in a world of their own, romantic by the very nature of their existence, yet lethal to the traveling naïve. They are more impressive standing by themselves in the wilderness than any man's imagination can construct with skyscraping knockoffs. Concrete, glass, and steel is how we imitate God's natural creations, but we don't even rate when it comes to this glory.

I had only slept about ten seconds on the plane flight in from Dubai, so I drifted back to sleep in my opulent, business class seat, satisfied that I had finally made it through my life to see the Himalayas at last. The next little nudge I felt was the pretty Nepali stewardess interrupting my unhurried dream. I was on a hallowed trek through ancient, distant villages, and, as a die-hard romantic, I envisioned rendezvous' with all sorts of pretty athletic sweethearts vying for my affections —

"We're on final approach, Mr. Dormire, seat backs up, sir." I kindly thanked her with a nod, trying in the next moment to desperately remember the spirited brunette who'd teased me along the trail in my dreams. Our Gulf Air A330 Luxury Transport bounded off the runway, taking the entire stretch of the haggard tarmac to come to a stop. We actually porpoised up and down with a slam much like I neatly accomplished during my tiny Cessna lessons as a bright new pilot. Oh, how our memories bring us back to the splendor and recollections of our sketchy past. I wondered if we weren't going to skid off the runway into some field and explode in a fiery mess.

We shuttered to a controlled rollout and the big airliner had to use the entire teardrop turn-around at the end of the runway to back-taxi to the terminal. I looked out the side window as we passed other large transports already parked on the apron. They too, no doubt, had to cool their own brakes from slamming them to a stop inside the thresholds of the small Nepali strip. Then we passed the fleet of tourist aircraft that would take trekkers by the plane load (cattle wagons) up into the mountains above.

I could see the Dornier and DeHaviland turbo prop transports loading the first morning trekkers for the trip into the various mountain states. These travelers were bound for one of the different regions above; Everest, Annapurna, or the Pumori, Langtang, and Doplo ranges to the west. Their twin engine aircraft lined the short-field parking in even angles adjacent to the domestic terminal where I'd be moving through tomorrow. But for now, I was soaking up every bit my solitude as we taxied in to park, realizing that for the first time in over seven years, I was going on a vacation by myself.

The Kathmandu airport terminal building was made of deep red brick and corrugated aluminum siding as roof panels. The primitive buildings off the edge of the runway that surrounded the airport were the raised apartment houses of a sprawling ghetto. Each one was stacked upon the other in haphazard rows. Some houses dotted the rolling hills and climbed above the city in terraced layers. Other shanties weaved into the lush, green jungle that dominated the origin of the city landscape. They spread for miles in every direction like the petals of a dusty, wilted flower in a full, but unkempt garden. There was no guessing about it anymore; I had made it to this part of the planet for a visit. I was fully attending my senses that morning, and this was Kathmandu, gateway to the Roof of the World.

As I gazed over the ancient, 2500-year-old city awaiting my arrival, I knew with every fiber of my soul that before I even got off the airplane, I wanted to come back.

Our welcome greetings were heralded at the bottom of the aircraft stairs by a young Nepali girl handing us their ceremonial shawls. Like Hawaiian leis only silkier and without the flowery display, this traditional ensemble, I learned, was given to all honored guests. Of course, their hospitality extended to every lowly tourist as well - *which meant me* - and each scarf was handed to us with a genuine, appreciative smile.

"Namaste," she said, which basically means, *I salute the Godly spirit in you.* I clasped my hands in prayer in front of my chest and returned her greeting with a nearly imperceptible bow, "Namaste." *I salute the Godly spirit in you, as well.*

When these greetings occur between two people, it seems that for one brief instant they are tied intimately and forever with each other's hearts. The love for humanity I shared with her in that moment radiated from both our eyes and smiles. It was like this with everyone who greeted me along this trip. Even the children are taught to send the traditional salutation to strangers as they pass. And without questioning any of its real significance, I would later be hailed by kids no older than three who would smile and give the heartfelt greeting, giggling and running along at their day.

Inside the tiled airport terminal, I paid for my entry visa at one counter, and picked up some chocolate filled wafers and a slender can of pulpy mango juice at another. The polished checkered floors and smartly uniformed crews of workers, baggage helpers, and passenger attendants were a direct contrast to the spectacle waiting for me outside. I moved to the public greeting area and met my tour company's owner, Ram Hari. He wasted no time in ushering me neatly to our car through the beggars and tour guide solicitors that smothered westerners coming out of the airport doors.

Along the terminal wall there were large banyan trees shading the cool, early morning air, with monkeys running along the sidewalks near passengers and people moving about in chaotic swirls. Cabbies who vied for our business were parked on a dirt patch not far from where we found our own driver and car. Street urchins selling small, colorful lanyard purses, and others selling beads and decorative necklaces swarmed us as we made our way. It was good having Ram with me, but I found that unless I motioned him to shoo them along, he let them offer me whatever they wanted. Their persistence rivaled even the most starving beggars from Calcutta to Morocco and everywhere in between.

The road from the airport to my hotel was a mix of broken cobblestones, dirty pot-holed asphalt, and an excuse for every crappy, smog-blowing vehicle on earth to come out and move around as fast as they could. Every inch of it was a haggard, rock laden maze of chaos and mayhem. Drivers and riders alike moved on the left side of the street, like the English do, or the Kiwis. Motorcycles split the center line by the hundreds, whooshing by in swerves one way or the other. For the most part, they avoided any disastrous entanglements with the mass of other stark raving traffic shooting by every one of them along the way. Scooters swarmed around people and goats and nearly hit most vehicles in reach, but didn't.

Dozens of motorcycle repair shops were open and already busy, clustered along sections of the sole, unpaved route we traveled toward the hotel. Bikes were laying on their sides in the dirt and being stripped for parts. Those on center stands had wheels, seats, or forks missing and some of the shops had close to a dozen bikes in various stages of disarray sardined into their tiny cement garage. I couldn't distinguish between whether this street was a sightseeing novelty, or the worst alternate route our driver could have selected.

Dallying in Nepal

There is no tax on motorcycles or scooters in Nepal so their abundance is stifling to an already congested city. Cars are considered a luxury and are taxed 140% or more over the base sticker price. This deterrent only slows the very poor, for the rest of society makes due with anything from big Mercedes to the smallest Chinese variants that could fit into the glovebox of the Mercedes if you really tried.

Suffice it to say that every trip I took through the city during my stay was an adventure of unknown proportion. Each move from one street to another held the dangers and thrills I would have tied to any crowded third-world marketplace. The insanity of driving uninitiated through the streets of cities like Seoul, Paris, or Rome, was like amateur hour compared to moving around in Nepal.

We swerved off the dirty maintenance road and onto a tourist shopping strip. Our speed was upsetting to me in the tight confines of the narrow pathway and we eventually squeezed into some alleyway that opened up into a blur of people, bicycle-rickshaws, and horns. I got dizzy trying to keep up with all the sights that spread in every direction away from the car. But before I knew it, there it was, the Tibet Guest House and café, the sanctuary I'd use for the duration of my visit in Kathmandu.

The eves of the four-story guest house were painted with a mixture of orange and teal laminate, and there was a bricked-in garden patio access up some steps just off the driveway with serving tables, a stone elephant fountain, and several guests ordering breakfast or tea. The main entrance to the hotel lobby was ornamented with intricate wood carvings of crowned deities, snake heads, and lions, all said to be guarding the hotel property from demons and pests. Tall porcelain vases flanked the entryway and they had brightly colored artwork depicting flowers and scenes of Sherpas and yaks with heavy bundles on high mountain walks. The arches and doors were a rich dark mahogany, big and heavy with round, brass medieval handles, and the whole structure left an appealing sense of authenticity to the well-traveled guest.

I was thinking to myself, *'Finally, I've arrived in a place that's for real'*. My room was a spacious third-floor suite with a clean private bathroom and open-walled shower - no curtain, just step over a hump and get wet. I was given some time to rest and freshen up but by midday, I'd met up again with my driver and we were off on a half-day tour of the city sights.

First stop on the schedule was the ancient, religiously significant Swayambhunath Hindu Temple in the upper-city hill district. It is popularly known worldwide as the "Monkey Temple." I found a full perspective of great pictures and animated descriptions inside the weblog, TripIdeas.Org, *(*http://tripideas.org/the-sacred-monkey-temple-kathmandu/*)*.

The 365-stair-step Monkey Temple, or *Guiasuri Shrine*, is a wedding favorite for happy young couples. From the two approaches to this inner-city summit, they climb the elongated stairs in hopes to please the gods and be rewarded with fertility and long life - a rather common theme of temple shrines placed inside the Hindu or Buddhist domains.

The center point of this monument was an ancient, dominant *stupa*. This was the name for any large cement oval-shaped crown that topped a series of steps on all sides and looked like a white upside-down salad bowl. In spiritual terms, it symbolized tiers of ascending platforms leading to the pinnacle of enlightenment - the goal of every good Hindu. According to their beliefs, it takes ages of reincarnations to reach the highest caste in heaven and share life forever with God.

Swayambhunath Temple Pagoda and Grand Stupa. Photo: B. T. Dormire

Instead of bounding up the multitude of off-angled steps, my driver wound us up around the easier route to park the car so we could get out and explore. At the top of the temple grounds, I looked at the stairs leading in from the other side and peered curiously down the hilly approach. Tourists, who felt like spiritual pilgrims on an afternoon's intrigue, labored up the wide cemented staircase under all shapes of overhanging banyans, giant bougainvillea, and small deciduous pines.

True to the name - Monkey Temple, there seemed to be dozens of large furry Rhesus monkeys taunting the visitors for crackers and handouts of nibbly peanuts or dried fruits. They appeared gangly in the trees and could have overwhelmed the unsuspecting travelers had it not been for the local guides who treated the monkeys like revered, but forlorn pets. The active primates certainly caused their share of mischief, but a quick, fun holler from the tour providers and the monkeys cowered back onto the safety of the higher, larger branches of the trees.

I spent a few minutes taking pictures and admiring the artwork of the prayer stones and the temple architecture. I watched the priests and tourists mingle under intricate wooden carvings. These tiny, white structures made up the numerous shrines for locals who, unperturbed by the visiting throng, thanked the particular god of their daily need (health, luck, prosperity, or fertility). To validate their pledge to serve their merciful deity, they brushed a red tikka dot with their thumbs to their foreheads. I left this first shrine in the purest, most authentic of earth's countries with a renewed sense of splendor that as poor as these people were, they were happy and fulfilled in their spirits unlike any of the dynamic, progressive cultures of the West.

Then the real poverty set in. The beggars on the path back to the car were shocking to me. I passed a man so frail, that he couldn't have weighed more than forty pounds fully clothed. A young mother, just as tiny, was breast feeding a little baby and had her hand out for any of my spare dollars or rupees. I barely got back to the car as the vision I'd pictured of begging multitudes from the most depraved Indian slums began to mass around my initial gesture of western benevolence. I was a little put off by the fact that my driver had gone on ahead to let me fend for myself. But it was an unkind lesson that I had to learn - don't get emotionally caught up in the poverty of millions. A thought swept over me, *Save who you can if they come, but save yourself as well.*

We drove back down the hill and headed to the famed Thamel street market. Freak Street is what some have nicknamed it and this was no less a manifestation of every other drama I'd witnessed thus far, and we hadn't even finished the first day. Scores of vendors had their wares spread out on blankets with everything from brass figurines to wooden carvings of sensuous adults embraced in the act of love.

Apparently the Hindus worship fertility and virility in many forms and this leads to big families and prosperous domains. There's even a god and goddess of love - *Kamadeva* and *Rati.*

These deities of pleasure and virility along with many of their phallic depictions are carved into 700-year-old temple architecture. The internet encyclopedias explain that the male figure, *Kama* translates from Sanskrit as:

> [S]exual desire, pleasure, sensual gratification, sexual fulfillment, or eros. It can also mean desire, wishes, passion, and longing; pleasure of the senses, the aesthetic enjoyment of life, affection, or love, all without sexual connotations. The female name *Rati* in Sanskrit means the pleasure of love, sexual passion or union, amorous enjoyment, all of which Rati personifies."

Other merchants sold scarves and dresses, robes, beads, and highly ornamented silk and alpaca kurta-surawals, a sort of casual pant dress familiar to women and comfortable to the touch.

There were beggars of other extremes in the midst of Freak Street. Unsightly and deformed humans of both sexes wandered or crawled the darkened alleys and lay along the sewer conduits. These were 'the untouchables', as my driver explained - the lowest caste of humans on earth. They were either punished in karma from a previous deed, or they were now ascending from the insects or animals to a better life yet to come. Some used canes or wooden crutches carved from a tree. Some needed leather or tire remnants on their hands and leg-less torsos to twist their agonizing bodies from tourist to tourist. Some writhed or dragged themselves along the dirty streets reaching out silently for help.

This existence was incomprehensible to me, for on occasion, a decrepit, wandering eye still full of intelligence caught my own. Something that signaled to me that these creatures had cognizance, that they knew they were crippled and this was their lot. My faint acknowledgments to them got easier as I moved deeper into Thamel Square; the look of an unafraid stranger was the only joy they ever received. I was able to avert my revulsion and pretend they were simply misshapen souls from another time and place, and I accepted them for who they were. But as I walked through the depths of their sprawl and from somewhere deep in my heart, I heard the wails of the Taliesin Orchestra playing *Adagio for Strings* over and over again in my head. I admitted to God that I was thankful I didn't have to live this way myself - at least not for this go around on the earth.

Freak Street, it was said, held some prominence in the sixties and seventies. The likes of the Beatles, Bob Dylan, and the Rolling Stones frequented the Haight and Ashbury-esque club scene of this part of Kathmandu that ringed the market square. I could see why they'd come here; the lure of discovering anonymity again was much too great to ignore. Life was simple in the lash of excitement of Thamel Street. Anything away from the paparazzi, screaming fans, or never having any private interludes again in open cafés was a joy. I thought on their behalf, *there are no strangers in Kathmandu, only people who've never seen you before.* Despite the impoverished conditions all around the rock n' rollers of the age, it was hip to survive the hashish dens and Hindi influences that left impressions on so many musical themes.

Back in those days, Nepal's royalty was tied to King Birendra and Queen Aiswarya. Before their murders by the deranged Prince Dipendra in 2001, the palace grounds bordered Freak Street and the market area of Durbar Square. Many examples of Buddhist architecture and Hindu temple shrines adorned the slum I was having a late lunch over that afternoon. The upstairs restaurant presented quite a vantage point for the spectacle and vibrant activity below.

It was easy to notice that in most of the temple grounds and bustling markets of Kathmandu, sacred cows were everywhere. They'd wander around, or just lie in a spot and relax. People gave them straw and clumps of grass or leaves to eat as offerings and there was no apparent logic connecting the beasts to an owner or a barn. They existed in a contemporary time line, treated like honored spiritual guests who are revered as a symbol of life, as the living sacredness of Mother Earth.

Hindu's don't actually worship cows as much as they respect the benefits of what the cows provide - milk and its byproducts, fuel from manure, and - just in case their late aunt or uncle came back as one - the cows were also regarded as an indispensable member of community life. A funny thing though, I noticed that each cow I passed was absolutely spotless. Their coats were healthy and clean, and there wasn't a speck of dirt or manure on any part of them. They were immaculate, chewing their cud and watching the throng.

The walk back to the Tibet Guest Hotel that afternoon was a cacophony of vehicle engines, blazing scooter horns, and clattering bongo trucks. Merchants were another distraction. They chanted for sales from their storefronts accesses, or pushed their arms full of trinkets into my face.

Bicycles and peddle-rickshaws had prayer bells that jingled more like bamboo mobile chimes on a windy day than any dainty charm. Sliding aluminum doors opened or closed at will with a deafening crash. The area's street dogs barked at everything that came within earshot. And wild monkeys shrieked high in the trees surrounding people gathering in the squares.

At that point, I was pretty caught up in all that was going on around me. It seemed like the deeper I got into the market alleys, the more traffic and people were jamming into the little spaces as well. Life itself was clogging the walkways like an overloaded funnel. It would have suffocated any normal tourist vying for solitude and for getting away from it all. Indeed, Kathmandu, or anything else about Nepal for that matter, was not a place for sissies. I must have been the exception for traveling without worry; I liked the bustle and chaos of its controlled panic and vibrant disarray.

When I got back to my room at the hotel, I rearranged my non-essentials for storage downstairs and loaded my pack with things I would need for the trek. I started thinking about the journey ahead. Contrary to my personal intrusion on these sacred lands, every seasoned westerner who came to Nepal was physically and mentally robust. Not only were they prepared to tackle the insurmountable challenges of trekking through Himalayan heights, but they were spiritually and financially determined to finish as well. People on serious expeditions, prepared for their adventures with thousands of dollars in gear and supplies. And they fortified their physical abilities to stay in the harshest environments on earth through their training and perseverance.

Invariably, at the end of each trip, two things would be set into motion with people once they were down from the peaks. The first came from some unwritten importance attached to buying last minute trinkets or strands of colorful jewels. These souvenirs held special reminders to people of their trek once they returned to the world.

Second, each traveler who labored on foot through the void above 12,000 feet formed their own answers to the *meaning* of life. Even enlightenment came to the lucky few. Some yearned for experience and found a spiritual peace instead. Some accomplished physical feats they never expected of themselves, no matter the phase of their trek. To finish a summit or not, some gained more by simply *experiencing* Nepal than anything else.

Bartering in a remote mountain gallery for a beautiful Himalayan painting held its own pleasurable significance. Others might prefer chanting OM's in an ashram hailing the perfection of life's unity. Still, the more practical visitors were just as happy recounting the in-your-face landscapes or dodging temperamental pack trains on a Himalayan switchback.

Everything that enhanced the spiritual upheavals for the newly initiated tourist proved that their journey to this land was something to value. For myself and the rest of the world's most naïve trekking upstarts, the trip of a lifetime was about to begin.

☯

Weathered Out and International Friends

Day 2 - 8 October, 2012

Kathmandu to Lukla.

At 5:30 in the morning on my second day, the Carlsberg beers I had at the hotel restaurant the night before were taking their toll. I woke up late and in my hurried state, I discovered that it took about ten minutes for the water to heat up in the hotel shower. By then, of course, I had elected to douse off in the cold in lieu of not freshening up at all and I'd just have to get over it.

Fortunately, I stowed everything I packed the night before, including my computer and excess luggage, with hotel security - if there was such a thing - anticipating our early departure. This saved me the time and headache of running around when probably everyone else was thinking the same thing, but waited till the last minute instead.

My breakfast consisted of a mad dash through the restaurant's buffet table as I loaded up on steamed veggies, glazed potato squares, corn flakes, and more mango juice than the day before. The mango nectar was becoming a growing favorite for me just two days into the trip. For the road I grabbed a hot, buttered slice or two of raisin-swirled cinnamon toast.

The owner of Shizen Treks, Ltd., Ram Hari strolled into the guest house lobby at 6:00 a.m. and spotted me finishing breakfast in the hotel lounge. He had my trek guide in tow and introduced us.

"Sir, this is Hansah Oksah. He will be the guide for your time in the mountains and is very experienced in the region where you are going. If there is anything you require, just let him know and he will see to your needs."

We shook hands with a warmth and sincerity that shown in his eyes and it put me at ease right away. Ram Hari gave him some trip money and dished out a few last minute instructions. Then Hansah and I got in the company car to catch our plane and took the narrowest back alleys and bumpy roads I think remained in all of Nepal. I asked more than once, "Is this the way to the airport?"

All I got were smiles from Hansah and the slightest impression from the driver that my questions bordered on the edge of being rude - but then again, not quite, it took a lot for these people to get upset, especially at the start of a brand new day. Well, *No harm in being cautious,* I thought. To my surprise we climbed rutted city hillsides I didn't remember passing on our drive *toward* the hotel the previous day. We raced a motorcycle through the darkness for a one lane opening off a side street onto the main thoroughfare - the motorcycle lost.

At unreasonably high speed, we circled a rotary near a shadowy market square. When we emptied out onto the main drag I could make out a long line of carts and tented kiosks with young merchants setting up their family's tiny businesses in the early morning dew. As we charged through the back streets and rut-strewn alleys, I began to feel that we were making some progress.

In contrast to the impoverished Nepalese masses striking out to meet their day, we passed a fairway or two of Kathmandu's National Military Country Club - their local golf course. As with any morning ritual associated with golf, the most serious duffers were out there warming up at the tee box before sunrise. Golf in Nepal, I thought, now that would be nice, maybe I'd try it. On second thought, maybe I'd leave well enough alone. I'm not sure I could handle a two-dollar-a- day caddy in shorts and flip-flops kicking my ass all over the course with a 3-under par.

Dallying in Nepal

The airport lay before us and we charged into the parking lot only to find a long line of trekkers had already formed at the entry control point and no one was getting in until the *Minister of Doorways* finished his tea and unlocked the gate to the security scanners. A sign of one of the local breweries above the entrance read, *'Be like the Mountains of Nepal. Stand Tall and Move Slow.'* Sound advice I thought, since we weren't going anywhere in this tourist logjam anytime soon.

From the first moment we were introduced at the hotel, I noticed that Hansah insisted on carrying everything I owned - even my hat at one point. Through the dirt-laden, airport parking lot to the lineup at the security doors, the determination and commitment he displayed for carrying all of my gear for the rest of the trip, included lifting his own bulky pack as well. I finally told him that I liked carrying my stuff. He quickly reminded me that he had just come off an arduous hike with 40 kilograms of gear through passes over 5,000 meters high - three days ago! "It's my job, sah," he said.

Damn it. I was pleased that the regard he held for his duty was so intense, but with the impasse, we finally agreed that I would carry my day-pack at all times and until we found the porter, we would work together to get the other packs loaded on the planes, taxis, or whatever conveyance we needed at the time. He was a small guy, maybe five feet, five inches tall and probably no more than 120 pounds soaking wet. But he was born a Sherpa and was strong as steel. All told, their lung capacity, as I would soon find out, was nearly half-again as much as mine.

To the people of Nepal, serving others is part of their religion. The care and nurturing of a fellow spirit is serious stuff to the Nepalese. To the majority of people in the west, living under the pretense of modern affluence and having some third-worlder wait on them hand and foot is a luxury they don't often receive. I'm not particularly sure about that edict, so I carried my own gear as long as I could get away with it, *even though Hansah was still biting at the bit.*

B.T. Dormire

The contracted Sherpas must laugh at the low-landers crowding their airport halls. Dreamers who want a glimpse at immortality trek for miles into the highest altitudes praying for good weather and good views of the Himalayan expanse. Some are blessed with these conditions and flourish off the success of their efforts. Some wind up being rescued off the mountain plateaus by helicopter, exhausted from muscular failure, altitude sickness, or the worse they could get, high altitude cerebral edema (HACE). That's the swelling of the brain due to lack of oxygen, (moving too fast up the slopes).

There are other messy sicknesses hovering in the shadows up there, but with normal precautions, say a regimen of charcoal tablets before landing in country, most trekkers come off of the slopes with plenty of stories and friendships collected along the way.

Inside the airport terminal, it felt like some of the guides were in hysterics pointing out their clients-of-the-week to their peers. Sometimes they broke out in hysterics, loving to make fun of their charges, or taking bets on who would make the climb to Base Camp without passing out or needing an emergency evacuation. I think Hansah was glad to see that I was in at least a fair amount of shape for our trek. I'd suspect he'd put his money on me to survive.

International contingents visiting Nepal were strewn all over the airport terminal. Pack flags identified most of the prominent groups inside the holding area as we readied for our flights. There were teams from Russia and Great Britain; athletes from Australia and New Zealand; all manner of Europeans, including the Swedes and the Nordics (*was there a difference in that genealogy?* I wondered). They were all aching to hike the great trails. There was even an American or two in the bunch - but not many. I was one of them, Rockies born and raised further out west near the Sierras.

A couple of groups hailed from Peru and Chile and they reveled in their own sense of accomplishment for mastering their climbs in the Andes. But they were here now and playing a whole new ballgame. They appreciated their mountains back home, but were visibly humbled by the fact that they were about to enter the big leagues. Even if most of them never set foot above 18,000 feet, it appeared that they were all here and ready to try.

The Orient was represented too; most of whom were quiet and reserved as always. They were striding around with their own separate confidence that came from thousands of years of inherited cultural significance. The Japanese, Korean, and Chinese groups all displayed the divine serenity of men and women determined, it seemed, to do one better than any of their international counterparts. Though everyone was cheerful to each other in passing, you could feel their edgy, competitive natures simmering like a brewing stew.

The terminal was packed with people hoping for their own inkling of importance. They longed to be in the same class of men and women whose mountaineering feats were inexorably tied to their lifetime achievements and forever stand the test of time. Experienced trekkers knew what the rookies had yet to understand - *plod on and never give up.*

Could these newbies remain as dauntless and fearless while securing their own uninitiated goals? Might some weary climber, or curious novice crest the Cho La pass at 17,000 feet and not be a different person for the experience? Would they summit Gokyo Ri and Kala Patthar and look up to see Mount Everest with the same awe and perspective as legends did before them? Could Sir Edmund Hillary have seen the same exact view on his way to the top, leaning against the same big rocks that were propping men up years after his original ascent, breathing fire out of their lungs and taking in their own series of heart stopping inspirations?

Thinking about the poignancy of that daydream alone, prompts thousands of visitors to get to Nepal in the first place. I was one of them.

Hansah strolled up out of nowhere and informed me that we were slated to leave on Agni Airways for a 9:30 a.m. flight in a long line of flights that would brave the Lukla high altitude airstrip. Built on a unique fingered plateau between two mountain peaks, Lukla sits on top of a cliff. It rests over valleys on each side of the approach and watches over a deep river gorge perpendicular to the runway.

I was told we have to fly to a point where we bank in with a hard 90-degree turn between these peaks and then fly *uphill* the final distance to make our touchdown on the short field strip. Legend has it pegged as one of the top ten most dangerous airports in the world. Its ominous stature rising and falling in significance depending on the amount of fog or clear mountain views a pilot ventures to try.

Lukla Airstrip, Cliff at far end. Photo at back wall: Byron Dormire

Of course, with any moment or temperament from which the mountain prevails, it will always have the final say. *But that's why we're going*; I told myself in a reassuring light. Lukla is just another part of the trip. "Stay close, sah," Hansah said. "We should be getting the boarding call at any time."

Just before noon, our flight had already been delayed twice. We were waiting on the weather to clear up in Lukla, and others going to Base Camp were stuck as well. Those heading for Annapurna and regions further to the west were moving steadily through the gates, thinning out the terminal to a more comfortable degree. The Finnish contingent took off in a private charter, but an hour later returned. Many more were to come and go. A team of French women were making themselves a place to sleep on the terminal floor - waiting patiently for the duration of the many 'Go, no-go' calls from the service carriers. Apparently, they had been through this before.

~

As I sat and waited for my pre-boarding call from the Agni-Air manifest, I began to reflect again on why I came to the Himalayas at all. The purpose of my trip, I determined, was initially two-fold, a third reason I'd get into later. The first was to simply accomplish the act of seeing these mountains in person; to take home a sense of wonder that such a place existed not only in reality, but in spirit as well.

The other purpose was to venture far from the confines of my familiar world - *and beliefs* - and seek the spiritual reckonings of a completely different cause - I wanted to outline a book on the missing life of Christ between His 12th and 28th year. I was there to research the possibilities of His visits to Tibet and Nepal.

In the translated works of Nikolas Notovitch from his book, *The Unknown Life of Jesus Christ*, myth has it in his 1894 treatise, that Jesus ventured through Afghanistan, Pakistan, India, and other areas 'east into the mountains'. Notovitch contended that Christ was on a quest for spiritual affirmation. That any need to free people from their earthly sufferings, eternal damnation, and never-ending misery, was meant to parallel the offerings God had already created for inner and outer peace.

Christ lived to perpetuate the glory of God for all mankind.

If the stories of his travels were true, Nepal could have been the closest he'd come to experiencing an authentic earthly place. He may have discovered more about the teachings of human tolerance and compassion through the examples of the people he met along his journey.

One such passage in a torn fragment of a sacred Tibetan scroll revealed by Russian archaeologist Nicolas Roerich says, "The farther, higher, and more revered *Jesus* climbed into the peaks, the more each of *His* steps glowed in the rocks."

Lady Henrietta Merrick confirms the existence of the writings in her book, *In the World's Attick*, published in 1931. She agrees that once aligned with the nature of his true calling, Jesus, who is named *Issa* by the Muslim Arabic faith, returned to his homeland around his 29th year to begin the tracks of his ultimate ministry - saving mankind from itself.

I set this second goal in motion from the moment I arrived: to gather information about the culture and environment Christ may have traversed. I wasn't necessarily seeking written or testimonial evidence of his existence in the Himalaya, just measures of what he could have done or seen if he traveled through these lands for himself.

~

I got up and stretched and then walked over to see the takeoff schedules for the different carriers. Their agents were manifesting passengers from previous cancellations by bumping and re-booking flights as the afternoon rolled on without any notable momentum – *not a soul was leaving the terminal.* It was 2:30 that afternoon and my guide kept strolling back and forth from the visits with his pals. None of them looked very assured pacing the terminal floor. Others appeared distressed as well, calling their tour planners and wondering, like me, when the cancel notice was coming or whether we were leaving at all.

I took it in stride and made the most of the lulls. I noticed the various expedition companies and was humored by the names on their bags. There were the pack groups of Peregrine Adventures, Exodus Climbs, and the Three Sisters Mountain Tours - an all-women expeditionary service that catered to female clients wanting to explore the distant reaches of Nepal.

There were the air service names as well: Yeti Airlines, Buddha Air, Agni, Tara, and Seta Air Transports, all displaying clever little logos tied to their themes. They flew people to the farthest ramparts of these mountainous meccas for treks, climbs, or photo-shoots. Commercial advertisers dropped in out of nowhere with beautiful people contracted to model gear and furrier brands in the most desolate places they could find.

I must have seemed an oddity to others standing around by myself. In fact, I think I was the only American left in the whole terminal which I thought was probably nonsense, but it might have been true. The Chinese group of about fifteen sat in the middle of the floor and had a late lunch with bowls of soup and crackers. The Brits took the chairs around a table and passed out what appeared to be champagne in oversized Dixie cups, tossing cheese strips back and forth between each other.

Pigeons were perched above the terminal hall on ledges and seemed to enjoy observing people going through dizzy human rituals. Between talking in excited, animated exasperation, and slumping in the hard plastic seats in total boredom instead, they must have been a sight.

Local travelers who were dressed in saris and Aladdin jammies filtered through the turnstiles to places aiming south. The planes were flying for the locals, it seemed, but they weren't flying northeast for any of us at all - not just yet anyway.

I took a breath, turned, and was completely surprised by a beautiful woman standing right next to me. No more than inches away, the slender blonde was looking into my eyes. "Are you that movie actor, Dennis Quaid?" she asked, pointing at me with a smile. I had to laugh; I got a lot of that. I don't see the resemblance, but I guess others do.

"No, my name is Byron, and I'm from Colorado."

"Hi Byron, I'm Kate Summers, from Queensland," she said with a cheerful Aussie accent. "I've seen you here all morning and I've been wondering about that. Are you trying for Lukla like everybody else?"

"Yes, I am. But unless a noted Swami flies in here this afternoon on a magic carpet and takes us all up there at once, it doesn't appear to me like it's going to happen at all. I think I'm trying again for tomorrow. My guide is already arranging our return to the hotel. Were you on the early schedule this morning, or more toward flights after lunch?"

"We were supposed to have left at 6:30 this morning," she said. "But our new flight leaves in a few minutes and they say we might make it under the weather, so we are going to give it a try."

Kate had a glow about her that was radiant and happy, and her strong, genuine features had a special appeal to me. Her high cheeks and strong jaw complimented her intelligent demeanor. Those blue eyes of hers and bright white teeth, they were magnetic to anyone who cast her a glance. It was like she knew something other people didn't - that she was full of spirit and love - and she might be willing to share it with whoever asked her first.

Feeling strangely disappointed that I would probably never see her again, I nodded my approval and said, "Well then, good luck to you and your group, Kate. It looks like my flight is about three hours behind you. If they're going in any kind of order, I won't be there until tomorrow for sure. How far up are you hiking on your trek?"

"We're going to Base Camp," she informed me with an infectious grin. I glanced down her figure for what I hoped was imperceptibly just an instant and tried imagining what condition her legs were in to make such a punishing climb. "It's going to be very nice," she added.

I had to agree. I said goodbye and waved to her as she

looked back at me once more through the holding area glass. I wondered, offhandedly, if I'd be arrested for barging my way in there without a ticket and slipping her my email.

Hansah startled me when he grabbed my arm and said we were going back to the hotel. "The flight has been canceled, sah," he said. So we gathered our things and walked out the airport's front doors.

We bounded back along the road in the taxi and I stared off between smoky buses filled with tired, smiling people. Girls sitting sidesaddle on motorbikes were heading home from work with their boyfriends at the helm. I wanted to kick myself for not running the gates before Kate walked out of my life for good. With a frustrated sigh, I still had hope that if I was lucky, I might see her again on the trail.

Before parting for the night, Hansah told me what time we were to meet in the morning for our next try up the mountain. I settled back into my room before dinner and jotted my thoughts in a small leather notebook I used to record the experience.

Soon enough, I ventured out for food and found the narrow streets and bustling storefronts just as intimidating in the dark as I had ever found them during the day. Again, it would be easy to get lost here because you take one wrong turn or another and it's like flailing inside a spider web where nothing is orderly and you're caught and claustrophobic. I thought for a moment that at least the spider *(or neighborhood locals)* knows exactly which way to turn. What a comfort for them, I imagined, not so much for me.

I made my way past art galleries and bead shops to a shirt store where they wove pashmina scarves and wool purses. One man was weaving the silky kurta-suriwal (utility skirt-pants for women) and asked if I needed any for a loved one back home. I said no thank you - *for now* - and strolled a little further down the alley to a busier part of the street.

Finally, I came upon a Korean *cheiktan* - (family restaurant), and dove right in. After living near Seoul for a couple of years, I knew what I was looking for with their traditional entrées. I had the *Bi-bin-bop*, cooked vegetables and rice, and they did a good job with it; though I couldn't see a Korean chef back there to save my life. Apparently, the Nepalese are great imitators, so I guess *simulated* authentic Korean food was the meal for the night.

On the way back to the Tibet Guest House I had a small negotiation between two store merchants over a packet of wet-wipes. I finally settled on the ones originally offered me by the Sari girl with the rings in her nose connected up the side of her cheek to her ear. Somehow she was especially enchanting to me, but maybe because by the end of Day 2, I was tired, alone, and ready for bed.

Falling asleep, I think I was still enamored with Kate and the way she walked away from me with a wave. "I'll see you, Byron *Quaid*," she said, as she stepped briskly through the air terminal doors and into the big, new world.

❂

The Treks, a Span Bridge, and Three Sisters

Day 3 - 9 October, 2012

The morning wake-up came with the shrill of my portable alarm and the simultaneous ear-shattering, old-style, dialer phone ringing in my room. It was 4:30 in the morning! "Wake-up call, Mr. Dormire," said the overnight clerk with a spark of humor in his voice. Crap! My head was pounding and I wanted to go back to sleep.

I managed to grunt something of a 'thank you' back at him like you might hear in a bathroom after a great Italian dinner. But with a 6:30 aircraft takeoff on a specially requested charter flight to Lukla, I had to get going by 5:10 if I was going to make it all.

I was in for another hearty drive over early morning roads. It was still dark out and we were narrowly missing the early risers traveling on foot or tootling along on their rusty bicycles. They darted in and out of our taxi headlights as they headed for work. Other people walked the dusty streets toward the start of their day carrying a change of fresh clothes or their lunch plates wrapped in a scarf. I smiled as I saw a hint of the dawn edging itself into the eastern sky.

The early morning weather looked the same to me as the day before. The sun was reddening through swaths of clouds, knifing its rays along the horizon in the distance. With all of yesterday's canceled flights, it was a zoo trying to get through the terminal and checked in with the 6 a.m. rush. Both days' worth of travelers and their packs were over-extending the air carrier lines to capacity and the tension to get out was apparent. Those from yesterday resented today's passengers with a passion. The newbies were hogging the lines before anyone could redeem what they felt was their rightful place to leave first. Of course, those scheduled for today felt the same. *'Hey, they had their chance.'*

Ram Hari hedged the bet that our regular airline would be grossly overbooked or might get delayed once again. I did not relish sitting in there for who knew how many more hours for naught, so I was relieved to learn that we were taking a single engine charter airline instead. I was also informed that I would need to pay another $120 - times two, (one ticket for me, and one for my guide, Hansah.) The way I figured it, I was paying more money for an aircraft with *one less engine*. But I also gained a bird's eye view of flying into a questionably hazardous airstrip. So, one way or another, this airplane ride and landing was going to be a treat.

There were seven of us for the little plane, including the stewardess. After manifesting with the charter service agent who sat in wrangler jeans with a clipboard in his lap on the tarmac next to the plane, we took off into the cool morning air and lifted quickly above the brownish haze of Kathmandu. After lunging airborne into the low scattered clouds of the immediate vicinity things cleared and I could see the splendor of the rugged peaks nearby. Hundreds more stood proudly off in the distance, skirting the Nepalese border and spilling well into Tibet.

Lukla was indeed the gateway to the higher mountain realms, but we had to get in there first. There was no cockpit door on the plane so I was able to watch in awe as the runway came into view. It looked more like a postage stamp from this perspective than anything else - *and we were headed there to land*. Specifically, the danger of the airport's approach was its six percent uphill grade a pilot needed to maneuver in order to get the aircraft down and stopped. Sheer momentum would slam it into the cliff at the top of the strip if it didn't.

As I looked up between the seats, I saw rugged forests on all sides of the landing site and the slope was getting awfully big in the front window of the plane. The optical illusion was as if we were aiming perpendicular to the ground, not parallel as an expected sight picture might normally display. By aiming straight towards the runway center-line, it looked like we were heading in for a controlled crash. It was definitely the strangest landing approach I've experienced for a while - maybe ever.

We taxied up to the passenger drop-off area near the terminal, probably because we were the first ones to land for the day. I guess the other carriers figured if we took first dibs at being the sacrificial goose, we could test the waters before anyone else and let them all know later if things were safe or not. More airplanes would follow, of course, and it was interesting to feel that we had led the initial flights to the mountains that day without a hitch.

As we stopped and the pilot throttled back on the prop, it felt like we were being ceremoniously dumped off at the passenger apron with all our gear. *"Dom dey Vadd,"* they said. 'Thank you very much, everybody. Now get out!' I knew they were just exercising their quick turn-around option for the first lucky passengers heading back to Kathmandu. There wasn't three minutes between our complete removal, the new group's load-up, and its departure again off the end of the runway. No sooner had the aircraft dropped off the edge of the cliff and disappeared from sight, than another inbound transport came into view to take its place. One after another, the new arrivals weaved in against the steep forested backdrop and flew down the treacherous glide-slope to land all over again and discharge their treasure.

Crowds of hikers and interested locals liked watching the aerial circus taking place off the distinctive, narrow strip. They gathered around the airport perimeter by the dozens to watch the new arrivals, and apparently this was some sort of everyday, ritualistic event.

The first thing I noticed in the mountain stillness between landings was the long line of porters-for-hire waiting outside the terminal fence at the airfield barrier. At least fifty of them were hoping for an impromptu pick-up of some lonely hiker. Or, they waited patiently for their actual clients who should have been there yesterday - *like me*. Nearly every trekker is tied to a mountaineering company with the contracted services of a guide and/or porter as part of the deal. The tour services from the capital usually arrange to offload packs and people, and they provide opportunities for the average porter braced against the fence-line for some sort of paying job. Sometimes a straggler flies up unannounced and this opens the opportunity for one of the male or female hopefuls to acquire some work.

There must be a sort of inborn radar the Nepalese have for each other, because out of all the Sherpas standing in front of me, Hansah spotted our porter at the back of the crowd. With a subtle, customary *'Gotcha, let's meet over there'* wave, most of them were in shorts and t-shirts, some wore sandals, and a few weren't wearing any shoes at all. Our young man was dressed in good hiking shoes, Dockers-type slacks and a nice clean red collared polo. We made our way to a reception area in a lodge that overlooked the airport to formally meet and divide up the gear.

The little gentleman we acquired was none other than Furbar Tahman, and, as it turned out, his family ran the lodge we went to for rest. We found he was an eighteen-year-old rookie porter and that I was the first trekking assignment he ever had. His uncle was a respected elder in the village who also managed the air scheduling times for all the carriers diving in and out of Lukla. Furbar's family seemed all teary-eyed that he was actually going out by himself on a trek with a paying client. He was lucky that I was his first, my pack wasn't heavy, I wasn't an asshole, and Hansah took him immediately under his wing with some of the best mentoring I'd seen for any new recruit. I too was glad we could break-in somebody new.

As for myself, I understood the daunting responsibility of tackling things as a beginner. I'd often lunged into solo scenarios for which I was unsure of or ill-equipped. From controlling guard observation positions as a site manager in a cross-fire gun battle in Iraq, to jump mastering parachute teams under squirrely winds into tight airshows or stadium crowds, sometimes I just had to wing-it, make things happen with a proverbial song and dance.

I could tell Furbar felt a little intimidated starting out on his first trek with an Alpha-type American. Though I was light on my feet and feisty, I was not in any hurry to scorn him for mistakes. However, before we launched, I had to adjust his pack harness straps to redistribute the weight. He had the bulk of it chomping down on his shoulders instead of his hips. That would have lasted him about ten minutes and he'd be hating life. Once we tightened and fastened the hip-belt, I think he appreciated the extra help in getting things started on a more comfortable note.

Furbar had a bright, round face, well-groomed black hair, and his wide eyes had the constant gleam of a permanent smile. He'd grown up as a happy kid and I knew this would give him many cheerful wrinkles as he aged through the years. Like most of the Nepali workers before him, he was diligent and took instruction well. Before we set out, his mother came over to see us off. She doted over him and said something under her breath that must have meant to behave. He smiled and shook his head yes. She gleamed back at him and cuffed his hair and was beautiful when she did it. I've noticed that every woman is lovely when they smile. I gave her a reassuring nod that Furbar would be okay. And he would.

The morning was in full swing and it was time to start our journey up the trail from Lukla. Hansah and Furbar were busy talking and had already checked the map. As I made my way down the stairs from the family's lodge, I strolled out on the walkway leading to the cobblestone alley. From here, I turned left into a narrow section of shops that led past a mountain supply outfitter and standing there right in front of me was Kate! She'd been checking on some gear and bumped straight into me coming out the door. It appeared she had a habit of popping out of nowhere and I was always being surprised by it. She had a big smile on her face, fresh and perfectly inviting when she said, "Well, well, if it isn't my hero, Sir Edmund Hillary."

My laughter was hearty and infectious. I hadn't remembered feeling so invigorated by a woman for quite some time. I made a surly observation, "I can only hope that this get-together is because you want me to personally carry your pack to Base Camp."

She laughed. "No, no. They were sewing my jacket here, but I was trying to find a little Bavarian bakery they said was around the corner and I saw you at the top of the stairs. Anyway, what *would* you charge to porter my luggage? I've got a dozen new shoes I need carried to the top."

I was shaking my head like I should have expected no less. She was quippy and smart. I looked up the alleyway toward the trailhead and spotted Hansah who had turned toward me for a signal on what to do next. I held up my hand that I might be a minute and he understood. Kate and I found the German pastry shop she was looking for and we had fresh baked croissants and some mountain tea. We talked about a few of the sights in Kathmandu we'd already been to, butchering the names of the shrines and temple monuments as we did. We could only venture to guess what we might see ahead on the trek.

"Kate, I hate to seem rushed, but I think my guide wants to get going. We're stopping a little further than Phakding tonight. He wants to go another mile or two before we find this special lodge he has picked out - some exotic brothel, I suppose."

She was shaking her head now. "Your choice of quarters sounds captivating. It would be nice to hear if you survive your stay there at such a high altitude."

"I know this might seem forward of me right now," I said, "but could I get your email address? I doubt if I'll see you again but maybe I could drop you a line for a nice 'hello' after we've survived our adventure."

She looked at me pondering whether I was a train wreck heading at her full speed, or someone she might like as a friend. I continued with a little banter like it didn't really matter either way; she was nice, but I wasn't here to find a wife. "You know, maybe we could compare notes once we get back to the world? Maybe buy a beach villa somewhere or a house?" I added this as a little flirt, casting it out there like a trout line into a state hatchery pool of hungry fish.

She seemed more curious than troubled. "Ah, I'm sort of going with someone, Byron. But maybe if I see you later, we can talk about this villa of ours." She smiled. "For now, I think you better be on your way." She pointed at my crew as they had crested the village lip and stopped there to wait.

"Okay. Sounds like a plan," I said. "Take care on your hike, Kate. Have fun on the trail."

"You too," she said with a comfortable look. "I'll see you later." She turned and headed back down the path, stepping with what I imagined was a little bounce, suggesting maybe that something else was in store for us down the line.

When I caught up with Hansah, he was looking at me with a smirk. For a second, I felt like I'd just been caught running my finger through the frosting of a cake. I smiled and told him to keep a look out for her because if we passed her on the trail and he didn't tell me about it, I'd throw the lavish tip for his expert services right out the window. His now familiar response to my critiques, complaints, observations, or ambiguities was very accommodating. "Thank you very much, sah. Thank you very much."

~

I was stationed at a NATO site in the basin of the Kabul Valley surrounded by the brown, jagged mountains of Afghanistan. Each morning I'd look off across the sprawling, valley landscape of

Kabul and wonder about climbing their summits. The tall Koh Paghmar range to the west or the deadly Koh Kamaris due south, stand with their war-torn peaks majestically off in the distance. But we can't go near them. No one can. Land mines and insurgent hideaways forbid any honest appreciation of the rich culture and heritage these people could share with the world if they tried.

One morning I ventured out with a Canadian patrol up a small mountain relic to our north. It was a great prelude to my larger climbs to come in Nepal, but I noticed something very interesting spread all over the side of the 8,300 foot peak. Tons of petrified wood littered every square inch of the mountain top, and from what I could see, it was everywhere along the range we were at. It had to be the remnants of a million-year-old primeval rain forest, a geologist's dream. Some of the trunks were as big as a couch and twice as long. Who knew what life they supported so many eons ago?

With this sojourn as my first to Nepal, geographic splendor and cultural magnificence was in front of me right from the start. There were thousand-year-old monasteries nestled into lush green forests. They overshadowed hidden river valleys where tributaries flowed like milk over deep granite riverbeds. The Doot Koshie river trail, for example, (the milk river as it's called - white in color), hosted a plethora of mountain villages set up exclusively for international hikers.

The mystic aura of the upper tea houses added to my suspicion that one single ethos evolved from all these foreigners when they entered this sacred realm - that we're all a bunch of mountain-lovers who stroll vis-à-vis with our own spiritual connection to humanity. I sometimes felt by walking through this place that it was more a haven to me than I could ever acknowledge back in the world. As far as trekkers understand, few people rarely speak about such loose, concocted affirmations. However, everyone feels akin to the spiritual liberation they see within themselves as they move deeper into the scope of Himalayan influence.

Author at a Mahni rock carving outside Phakding. Photo by Hansah.

Not far into the hike, I encountered a series of mahni 'prayer' walls - a kind of permanent, spiritual engraving carved into the rocky boulders or on flat, slated ledges above the trail. These inscriptions proclaimed a litany of psalms for the viewer such as long life, health and happiness, prosperity and luck. The edicts among them infer that life is sacred and remind the penitent and godly soul to be kind to all they encounter. Some of the carvings share lessons in which all our eternal spirits belong to the creator and that we will see him again if our life is pure and worthy. The prayers ask us to live a good life so that our journey through enlightenment to nirvana may be sooner than later, our incarnations fewer than more. I think to myself, *Damn, I might be stuck here a while.*

As the trail made its gradual ascent, I was intrigued by the intricate placements of the stone-made path reinforcements. Waist-high walls along the way had thousands of chiseled rocks that were jigsawed and wedged into perfectly locked positions. They helped support the trail against the great proclivity of natural erosion. Not only are the elements shielded from wearing it out, but regularly attended maintenance allows for the reinforcement of hardened footfalls on the steep grades for hundreds of yaks, mules, and daily trekkers who clamor up their sides, season after season, year after year.

The stacked pre-formed rocks served a myriad of other purposes as well. They anchored the span bridges to the mountain that held not only people who crossed at will, but also the yak/cattle crossbreed called jube-ques. Along with the small mule teams that walked unguided up and down the route, the small, rugged jube-ques were the backbone of the pack trains throughout the mountain valleys.

"Always stay inside the path nearest the mountain," Hansah would say. "And watch out for the horns," he'd remind me. The beast's sure-footedness rarely faltered on the steep up or downhill grades. And some of these rocky stair inclines were so demanding that they could startle even experienced climbers who came upon them on a hike. The jube-ques just plodded along, no big deal.

The Sherpas were the real wonder. Like my porter, these tiny guys were as tough as nails and would haul an average of eighty kilograms (180 lbs.) on wicker framed baskets seven-plus miles a day for about $2.00 a kilo. Their cargo varied from large, heavy propane tanks tied together on wooden slats, to dozens of live chickens stacked atop their shoulders already laden with cases of beer - or corn syrup, sodas, water, or jugs of cooking oil. *(I only offered my help to the guys with the beer)*.

The seasoned guides came through with large groups of trekkers heading further up the mountain to the higher, more treacherous camps. Porters would tie two of their guest's fully laden packs together and tarp them for staying dry in the rain. These human juggernauts used a small headband strap to lean into the climb. This supported the loads more from their foreheads and necks than their hips like the modern rigs of climbers with North Face carryalls, Deuter alpine rigs, or the Mountain Hardware expedition gear.

Every Sherpa uses ropes and roping ingenuity with nothing but sheer grit to haul these rickety wicker basket designs. The bin of each carryall is unique in shape, like a blunted-end funnel that harbors twice the amounts of weight distributed through-out the lower half of the pack. The lighter payloads are always at the top and the heavier, proportional supplies

The final surprise to me was their shoes - or lack thereof. Some of the older men wore sandals, some nothing at all. Some wore the cheap slip-on, camouflage Keds the Nepalese army issues their basic recruits for exercise. These, of course, had worn themselves out with holes, tatters, and torn rubber soles; and they didn't provide much support for a guy carrying the weight equivalent to a really fat man on his back.

I tried to be a little cheerful and say hello sometimes along the way, but lugging crap everyday up steep mountain grades just to make a living didn't really boost their sense of a good-natured talk. I got an occasional smile, but for the most part they just looked at me as if I was some kind of asshole. *Either help me or get the hell out of the way, you dumb son of a bitch.* That was sort of the look I usually received when I tried to strike up a thought. Nevertheless, their smiles endured. There was always a smile.

We ate our first lunch at what I might have called a Swiss chalet if we were hiking in Europe. This grayish-blue trekker's lodge was just across one of the many span bridges we had to brave during our ascent to Namche Bazar.

The 'Happy Mountain Cafe' was on a plateau in a grassy field, the back of which nestled up against a slope that went straight up into the clouds. Made out of large, stone blocks with ornamented gables and a light blue pagoda-style roof, I sat in an open patio that was rich in roses and wild yellow dahlias. There were blue hydrangeas around the stick-wire fence that seemed out of place, but they were blooming there in the columned sunlight like they'd been doing for a thousand years.

The constant clang of cow and prayer bells - which sounded more like sleigh bells to me - meant that we were never far from a jube-que or pack-mule convoy. Hansah, Furbar and I finished our mix of dalbat porridge which resembled and sometimes tasted like liquid clay. But today's thick noodles were in a creamy sauce, seasoned to taste, and our potato-vegetable soup went down smooth as silk.

Then from out of the quiet murmur of the river flowing in the valley below, I heard a distinct yelp from down near the bridge. I looked up to see one of the jube-ques pushing its way past a loitering gaggle of trekkers taking pictures off the rails over the deep river gorge.

One of the older men in the group was helping a pretty young woman to her feet. As I looked a little closer at the ruckus smoothing itself out, I noticed that it was none other than *Kate* being helped off her butt. She'd been knocked down by the 400-pound animal clomping over the bridge. She actually averted a real disaster by grasping the bottom of the span wire laced precariously near the edge of the cliff. The nervous oxen were still plodding by - *they had a damn job to do,* but they were also dangerously close to gorging the shaken tourists still clamoring to get off the bridge to solid ground.

I eased back into my seat and Hansah gave me that look again - *Maybe you should just go down there for a hug and kiss her 'till she's better.*

I smiled at him and laid a five dollar bill on the table for the three of us. We got up and donned our packs. By that time Kate and her entourage had arrived at the café patio, most likely to collect their wits. She noticed me readying my team and I could feel her wondering if I had, in fact, witnessed the little calamity she just endured. I had indeed.

As we passed each other through the little picket gate, I took the liberty to say, "Kate, you didn't have to wrestle any jube-ques to cross the span bridge to see me. I'd have waited here all day if I knew you were coming. I'd have also hired you a personal rickshaw, or helicopter, to get you from one side of the river to the other."

"Is that right?" she said. "Why don't you just have a steak dinner and a hot tea ready for me when I get to Namche tomorrow night and maybe I'll think about giving you the time of day?"

"Sounds like somebody's ready for lunch," I said. "They've got a great one here if you like eating spicy Playdoe, and you can probably get a band aid in their concession to put on your tail feathers after your little tussle at the bridge."

Now if there was any question that she left her sense of humor in Australia, I would have never guessed it. She asked, "Are you applying for the doctor's role in that scenario, placing a band aid on me where it matters most?"

"Maybe so," I acknowledged. "But if I take the job here at the picnic tables, it might make me blush with you in front of my guys. They really look up to me, you know, and that would take me out of character with them as some kind of natural born super hero. What if a Yeti ambushes us on the trail and I have to fight him off? After playing doctor with you, I might not be in the right frame of mind."

"Oh, I'm sure you'll do fine, Mr. Hero," she said smiling as she moved into the café yard. "I hear the Yetis around here play cards with people, you shouldn't have any problems."

"That's 'Doctor Hero' if you're introducing us to anyone. I'll keep a guard's watch on the trail ahead, Miss Summers, thank you very much." I noticed more red roses in the planter-box next to the lodge as I stepped out on the path. "Au revoir, Kate," I said as I tipped my hat.

She watched me stroll on up the trail. Before I got too far from earshot she'd walked back to the fence and called out to me, "Don't run off with any Yetis."

I glanced back at her, confident that I was going to get her email after all. "Have a nice rest of your day, Australia. Watch out for jube-ques." My guide and little Furbar just smiled and shook their heads as they walked on ahead of me.

~

After our first day on the trail, *Team Shizen* finally arrived in Monjo to stay for the night. This little village was located on a sloping hill where each block-built Nepali structure sat at different levels on a staircase switchback. We were about four klicks out of Phakding and the same distance yet to go for Namche Bazar. Staying in this particular spot was to further assist us with acclimation and it gave us a better headstart in the morning. A monster climb awaited us tomorrow with what amounted to being the first real push up into the remote Everest highlands.

Monjo was home to a little rustic place called the *Namaste Guest House*. Thao and Sofia Ruunah operated the tiny lodge with a staunch diligence, a good-spirited welcome, and a no-nonsense approach to dealing with unruly customers. I'd heard him chewing out someone when we first walked in. "This is not winter season here, we don't give things away!" I had to chuckle at that one. Thao Ruunah looked like a nice enough guy but it was clear that he wasn't going to take any crap from anyone, at least not while he had anything to say about it.

There was no heat in the rooms, only a pair of bunks and a small table with a candle for light. It seemed, however, that after a few minutes of moving around to generate a thermal envelop, one could eventually warm up and get comfortably down to their knickers. We got settled into our separate rooms, then met up in the teahouse dining area and got ready for supper. I made a few entries into my journal and sipped a can of orange-mango surprise. A cascade of rain began to hammer off the corrugated roofs throughout the little Monjo village. The wind and chill that followed certainly precipitated the room's wood burning stove for providing warmth and to heat the chai kettle getting ready for the night.

I looked around at the walls of the dining area and noticed an ornately decorated and colorfully balanced collection of calligraphy art, prayer tapestries, and brass vases and pots. The old iron hearth was the centerpiece of the room and burning brightly. It stood before the lacquered cedar tables nudged against wall-benches with sewn seat cushions and matching pillows.

The tables were covered in thick panes of glass and I wondered if they'd been brought up the trail by Sherpa or mule train. Tall windows adorned sections of every wall - *more glass* - and the Nepalese were big on framing pictures of their special guests. They loved surrounding their teahouse lobbies with the collective smiles and impressions of mountaineering legends and their accomplishments. Photos hung above the hard-wood walls and latched onto the rims of their hard-wood ceilings.

The simple kitchen at the end of the dining area had an efficiency about it that bordered on science. It too had a wood burning stove, cemented-in and attached to the wall, which Thao blew air through a long brass tube to reignite cooling embers. He had three pans going in different spots and rotated them in and out depending on the heat he needed to either boil or simmer the food. The sink was an old wooden trough, deep but water tight. From these nascent utilities, they could feed a room full of guests and never break a sweat. Though the couple scratched out a meager living there, they were happy, and they did so in the modest of settings. They even had a twenty-four day old baby to pamper while they tended to hiker's needs of every sort.

The Nepalese often questioned those who clamored up here all season, moving to and from the distant, unimaginable civilizations of America, Europe, Asia, or the spacious, developing regions of a new and curious Africa. Sometimes the locals wondered why all the fuss.

The lodge seemed very peaceful while we sat there alone and quiet. But the ambiance felt out of place to me. I gathered that another atmosphere was more suited to the small serving room. I pictured their wild lodge gatherings and the noisy celebrations of victorious teams who came through here every year, searching for, or bragging about the tough peaks above. I could see the Ruunahs hosting the likes of drunkards, philanderers, and tall-story prevaricators tripping endlessly through the guest house doors. One could easily tell that a vibrant, rambunctious life was frequently experienced in this room. I sat and wondered if anyone else was going to show for the night.

Before I could finish that thought, two groups of *women only* trekking tours tromped through the guest house entrance to get out of the downpour. The Three-Sisters Trekking Company had two separate ventures going through Monjo at the same time. In a chance reunion, two girls with their guide, Sahja were coming back down the valley from a robust trek up the Gokyo Ri mountain summit (17,685 ft., 5360 meters). Three more women with their guide Lorinah and their female porters were heading up the mountain, just like us.

These women were tough. They'd been hiking for days with the scarcest essentials and limited facilities. When they tumbled into the Namaste Guest House to keep from being soaked, the female guides kicked off their surprise meeting with rodeo hugs and engaging chatter. It was a festive night from that minute on. Young Furbar was dragged over and plopped down between the two Nepali women and he couldn't answer their questions fast enough, looking back and forth between them with a huge smile, his innocence boiling over as the women loved him up.

I was enthralled with the adventures told to us by the two seasoned women of the groups, Roza and Mirka. One day after they stopped at a village for lunch, their yak wandered up a mountain slope to graze. The only problem was that it took off with all their gear and they had to chase him over polished, million-year-old boulders and through ancient forested ravines to get it back.

During another instance, the girls had to engineer a crevasse rescue pulley to get their gear across a deep crack when a snow bridge dropped everything through a shaft on the Ngozumba Glacier. They asked about my work in Afghanistan and we talked about their homes in England and Japan.

The three other girls were Australian and gangly, and it wasn't long before they broke out a brandy snifter and we each nursed a shot or two out of plastic camping cups. This team spread their gear out on one of the tables and I made some rigging repairs to the tall one's harness pack straps. As the night wore on, Thao brought out samples of a pungent Nepali fruit wine, called raxi - hard core moonshine was more like it. It was circulated around the group - a *couple* of times - and things were pretty boisterous with Snickers candy bar wrappers being tossed about like ammo in an off-handed deckle war. There was a subtle, cross-table thievery going on all night as well. Barbecue glazed chicken, mutton nuggets, and the endless sugar treats were being plucked off adjacent plates right and left. No one ate their own little snacks. We just nibbled off each others plates – tribal style. *"Hey, gimme that!"*

The flirting and 'come-see-me-in-such-and-such-a-country' innuendos tapered off as the fatigue took its course with us all. Eventually, the girls slipped off to bed. I was still reeling in my thoughts about all that had happened that day and I was amply satisfied with the results. I was immersed in a culture and country that was proving more hospitable and agreeable to my personal life's philosophy than I could have ever hoped or imagined. I was seeing an authentic aspect of humanity in a genuine place on the planet.

As it grew very late, I helped clear a few of the plates for Sofia and washed some of the pans in their cold well water sink with a Brillo pad and soap. I actually had to pump the water into the basin with an old-time handle and spout. Sofia seemed a little unsettled having me invade her kitchen like that, but she couldn't very well do anything about it while nursing her baby boy in the little booth around the family's kitchen table. I threw a dish towel over my shoulder like a pro and she simply sat back and watched with a grin. She had a glow about her as the infant suckled her milk and a peaceful smile that would melt anyone's heart, especially mine.

I was cheerful and happy to be in that tiny lodge, talking and joking with Hansah about his job-well-done for the day, watching over me on the trail. Watching out for Kate.

I hadn't felt this welcome in a place in years.

☯

Part II: Under the Shadow of Everest

Does the great mountain know, or even care that we travel up its map-drawn paths to get a rare and lasting glimpse? Does it pose for us between the breaks in clouds, or toy with our searches with divisions of light and shadows through the trees of a forest glen? Does it watch over us in some laconic swirl of spiritual mysticism, handing lessons out for those who have trekked before us in good times or bad?

Is our success or failure measured by how high we climb to reach a summit, even if we don't quite make it to the top? Are we tested by how far we trek into the marrow of the earth's cradle, to stand next to God's throne itself - Everest?

Are the tremors I feel underfoot a sign of its impatience, the mix of rock slides or a snowy avalanche, somewhere up the distant trail? Is it waiting for me to call its bluff, taunting its charging boulders to catch me between the eyes if I dare? And is the aftermath a sorrow so profound that it's delivered to me in a hurricane of tears?

If I stumble on a pebble or twist my ankle on a wet, exposed root, weather-worn and reaching out for me along the open road, is this just a hint to keep me ready? Am I supposed to steel myself against a greater fall, say, the loss of a lover, or the sight of a village being swept from existence by the very rocks I've honored in my climb?

❀

A River, a Tremor, and an Isolated Heart

Day 4 - 10 October, 2012

The sound of the white river flowing past Monjo that morning gently nudged me from sleep. We were set high above a series of barley and cabbage paddies and I could see the early light shining on the highest peaks above our lodge. The beginning of a new day was slipping through the window and I couldn't have been more at ease.

Hansah and Furbar bunked in a different part of the lodge and though we chose to sleep a few extra minutes, our plan was to rendezvous for breakfast around 7:00. Sap-filled smoke from the wood-burning stove wafted around in a suspended bluish haze outside the kitchen window. The sweet, pine smell lingered in the trees and was a sure ringer that something delicious was about to get underway. Thao already had our omelets sizzling off the plate and he swung into the eating area with a stack of grilled bread (Nepal's version of toast) and a dish full of apricot jam.

We saw neither hide nor hair of the Three Sisters groups before we finished. They either left before we got up, or they were sleeping it off. No matter though, it was time for *Team Shizen* to launch through our first tough ascent - the climb to Namche Bazar.

Thao's lodge and teahouse was the last stop before the

tough ascent to come, and it provided us comfortable quarters and meals. Once we started our hike out of Monjo, which began docile enough, I found that the effort was slowly turning into a grind I was going to have to endure for hours. Within the first ninety minutes, we dropped down a long slope and passed through the Doot Koshie lowlands to rise steadily above the river and enter Namche's daunting up hill challenge.

At 11,500 feet, my breathing began to wither. For the first couple of kilometers, several villages along the upper path offered a resting point for drinks and temporary breathers. What was ironic was the notion that any civilized life could exist past the darkened pathways through Larja Dobhan - the trail's gateway to Namche's harrowing switchbacks.

The tips we got from other trekkers heading back to Lukla, was in fact, consistent and profound advice. "Go slow and take it one little step at a time." I've known this from years of hiking through Mammoth or the Collegiate Peaks in the Sawatch wilderness. But in the throws of acting out various mountaineering fantasies, it's always good to be reminded to take it easy – no need for a heart attack or a brain aneurism in the middle of nowhere.

We had followed the river from Monjo for a series of up and downhill lofts, many of which began and ended with little half-dome shrines and prayer wheels sprinkled along the way. A blessing at one of the stupas read, "Spin the wheel and purify your soul." My mental reservations were on the rise as each prayer wheel got larger the further we went. Like maybe they were trying to tell me to go back where I belonged, and never attempt to sully this God-blessed land with my vile presence again. Before this point in my hike, I'd felt strong and motivated, like I could go as far and as high as I wanted. Now I was beginning to wonder if I should have taken up shuffleboard instead.

From one spot near the river trailhead, I could see high up the steep ravine and how the path wound like a ribbon into the forest above. I caught sight of a mule train moving up the same route we were heading and I could see that we still had a long way to go. It was straight up and without a reprieve. It reminded me of a climb I've made several times in Manitou Springs, Colorado. That little amble is called, *The Incline*. On mornings that a hiker wishes to haul up the slope to watch the sun rise off to the east, he faces three-thousand railroad ties placed unevenly up the side of a vertical firebreak. It's a genuine leg-ripper and once on top, it crests to a point where the trail turns back down a path to the famed Cog Railway station in upper Manitou. The opposite trail continues to climb to Barr camp for a quick rest or to stay overnight. The more ambitious climbers go on to summit Pike's Peak from there (14,110 feet). A relatively humble march compared to where I was at in the Himalayas, but still respectably heartbreaking to the unprepared.

Naively thinking I could do anything I wanted overseas, I was enthralled with the prospect that I had arrived in-country fit enough to tackle whatever these peaks threw at me whenever they wanted. Then again, I was still meandering down at the river like I'd performed some sort of vast, egocentric achievement. I would soon discover that the *Incline* version of my Nepal ascent held four times as many uneven stone stairsteps as Manitou Springs.

Located at over 12,000 feet, Namche Bazar was a major Sherpa settlement and hub for expedition layovers, a primary altitude acclimatization point, and the main resupply center for those heading further up the trails. The overlooks at Gokyo Ri and Kala Patthar, and even Everest itself were destinations these climbers were heading. Though Namche was only about four kilometers in distance from the river's edge to the village above, it was a broken, gnarly scramble over uneven shale and rocks and the most difficult pitch for me so far.

Nevertheless, we went up there one step after the next. Steady but overheating, I was beginning to labor with increasing difficulty for the oxygen that thinned with every meter we gained. Constant sips of water kept my cotton-mouth in check and by hydrating so well, it increased my confidence that I might finish this trek after all. To do so without the embarrassment of throwing up was one of my primary goals. Another was not passing out from the exertion of my muscles screaming for help. Still a third and arguably the most sanguine reason to finish the climb, *which, if I hadn't, would have been a fate worse than death*, would have been giving up all together because the route was too tough for pansies like me.

For the first hour or so of our humble acclivity, I almost agreed with my own delusion that I might be good enough to go all the way. After the second or third hour of going straight up the side, I began to question where 'all the way' might be exactly - *my next step from a heart attack,* or maybe the Hillary Step on the last legs of an Everest ascent? There were lots of choices in between.

Dodging the sure-footed jube-ques that were passing me like I was standing still didn't assure my confidence that we were ever going to see the village summit. After a half a day of trudging far-reaching, mountainous switchbacks and dry-packed trail damage without so much as a break, I finally stopped for a rest. The altitude was beginning to take its toll, but it gave me a moment to account for where we had come.

I recalled that just past the Larja span bridge hovering high over the Doot Koshie river, we started up on our climb. Naturally the path just didn't ascend - that would have been too easy, too predictable for naïve, half-witted hikers like myself. No, this part of the trail had switched back *down* a vast, steep grade along the side of a cliff. Once we rounded the sheer face of a rock the size of a football field, the path started its way back up again through the trees. I looked above our position through the dense, overhanging foliage as it thickened before me, its shade now inviting me to get immersed inside the new experience.

I loved where we were headed, relishing the sights and smells of the approaching red rhododendron and wild magnolia blossoms. For some reason though, gazing through the shadowy overhang of dark, thickening trees, I couldn't help but feel a strange foreboding, like someone was reaching out to me and saying that I shouldn't go any further. For just a second, I felt a genuine trepidation in my heart, like something our beloved Bilbo experienced when he entered the Mirkwood Forest, that treacherous heaving of shadows and maligned spirits out of J. R. R. Tolkien's, *The Hobbit*. I kept hearing a little voice inside my head warning me not to leave the trail. *"Byron, don't ever get off the trail!"*

There had been a gurgling in my stomach for at least twenty minutes. By combining my fill of questionably nutritious food over the last few days without the luxury of a good bathroom to settle my woes, I suddenly discovered I needed an outhouse and there was nothing I could do to stop the gastronomical deluge from ruining my day.

"Hansah!" I yelled.

"Yes, sah!"

"I need a bathroom, man."

"Now, sah?" he asked kind of surprised and looking around like hell, what a dumbass, there aren't any bathrooms up here. Why didn't you go in the village we passed - *an hour ago?*

"I've got a problem, Hansah, and I need to go now!" I said as I tapped the back of my hips. I dumped my day pack on the retaining wall and started looking for an out.

"You need the Nepali system," he said as he pointed up the side of the trail into a thicket of brush. We had joked about this before. The Nepali system consisted of a private spot in the woods and a nice handful of leaves. Though I thought this image was hilarious a couple of days ago; right now it sounded like paradise.

I understood what I needed to do and my stomach was in no shape for debate. I started plodding up through the underbrush throwing off my jacket and vest. My abdominal pain was suddenly excruciating as I tried to hold everything back while I hurried to squat. Fighting with my belt and long underwear, I finally bounced off a rickety spruce sapling to lean against for a seat. I checked for poison sumac or the likes; (I had failed to avoid that experience with poison ivy a few years back and my underside exploded in fire for a week). Between the climb and the altitude, my legs were so fatigued that I could barely support myself for what was breaking loose in a malodorous torrential onslaught.

I think the worst part of needing an emergency bowel movement without a bathroom is conducting it in the humility of the open air. At this point though, I could not have cared less, and I was fairly content that I was in a secluded spot, privy to only myself and the little creatures of the forest looking on in obvious hilarity. But as luck would have it, I unwittingly set myself just below the trail which connected to the switchback *we'd be hiking over in minutes to come*. People strolled down this leg from above like it was a walk along 5th Avenue in Manhattan. Though they were polite enough not to laugh, I think they passed by me and sympathized with my plight. Everyone gets caught like this on the trail at one time or another. Unfortunately, from what I was experiencing at the moment, I knew I was going to be there for a while, *probably waving the whole time to passersby*.

The agony came from three places inside my body: the cramps in my belly that were tying my abdomen in knots, the burning muscles in my thighs causing me to tremble and sweat, and the worn-out knee cartilage I didn't help at all by coming on this trip. I was completely helpless while I stooped in a lazy catcher's stance, something that ruined my knees as a kid in Little League, let alone trying to repeat as a fifty-seven year-old tootling up and down the Himalayan countryside.

It was painful enough without having to worry about crapping in my shoes or down my pants which were drawn and clumped at my ankles, but now I was irked with concern. From out of nowhere, the flies began to arrive - big ones; shiny blacks and greens with their thousand little eyes bearing into me like they wanted me to die. Or if I wouldn't be that convenient, they were simply waiting for their turn at the trough. It was eerie watching their behavior, almost as if I could read what they were thinking.

They sat in a perfect semi-circle like knights at a round table, conferring about my fresh laid feces as some sort of grand dinner value they could tell their children about for years. All I had to do was tidy up and they'd finish off the rest. That's what I was thinking when I filled the haphazard hole I'd dug with dirt and tissues. I topped it with a bowling ball size rock, and spread Nepali leaves over it feeling sorry that I spoiled their fun.

The first, violent ground tremor hit when I was fastening my pants. I had almost finished when I noticed the shadows of branches moving above me without the help of the wind. I glanced up and the trees around me were wobbling in uneven patterns. Then I felt myself bouncing unnaturally in place, like riding out turbulence in an airliner speeding headlong through an ill-tempered storm. The quake stopped with one last, frantic jolt and I heard the grumbling earth beneath me settle back into a reasonably sober state, stilling itself to silence. I looked around and wondered if anyone else had felt what I just experienced. When I got back to Hansah and Furbar on the trail, it appeared they had not felt a thing, or maybe it happened so often up there that they took it in stride. I couldn't help but look up around me at the close, rocky peaks and wonder what might be haunting us from thousands of feet up.

I got back to the task at hand and we started off again toward Namche with another mile or so to go straight up the edge. I knew from my climbs in the States that anytime I got near timberline, my pulse had a tendency to hammer out of my chest once I topped 12,000 feet. Like clockwork, I could always tell where I was, altitude-wise, when the thought crossed my mind, *"I hope my heart doesn't explode on me here; I'd never get out alive."* I remembered to pace myself from my Colorado experiences and this set the tone for the balance of Nepal. The drudgery of step after step wasn't yet affecting my judgment, or so I hoped. The effort in this was never a breeze, but by accepting the strain from the very start, my life was much easier for me on this particular trip.

I remembered the first climbs of my youth, trekking

through high Sierra passes where I mentally quit long before my body actually gave out. Within each of those adventures, I had utterly failed to finish. Later in my military foibles, I learned through the harder climbs, that just the opposite had to take place. Mentally, I had to push my body farther than ever before, how giving out could only be justified as a matter of weakened physiology and ill-prepped endurance, not my psychological defect of quitting on the mission or failing in front of the guys.

Today, of course, quitting was a defeat against all levels of my personal philosophy. I needed the harsh stigma of ill-preparedness behind my previous mountaineering failures to achieve something more viable instead. The pressure of holding together a combined physical and mental endurance and never give up is always at risk. Even the enjoyment and satisfaction I got out of cresting each pass, topping each summit meant little if I had to be rescued or dragged off the slope.

Trekking in Nepal hadn't faltered my belief that I could go on, for I was still enjoying the climbs. I was putting one foot in front of the other and didn't hate every second of it while I did. The only relief I gained in these particular mountains - my saving grace so to speak - was the occasional village stopoff along the way. Grabbing a fruit juice or water, or chomping down on a quick Snickers every once in a while always hit the spot.

You had to pack your own goodies when you hiked in America. There were no convenience stores or appealing display cabinets on the trail over there. In Nepal, they had made it an art to accommodate every type of gallivanting tourist. From the pissy malcontents to the die-hard enthusiasts, no one was left unhappy on the great shleps over South Asian trails.

The going was rough now only because my ankles, knees, and even my hips were giving their all; biting at me from the jabbing impacts of this high-altitude trek. I was pleased, however, that my breathing and pace had stabled out and were not at their limits. My physical conditioning regimen back in Afghanistan had kept me from an early collapse, and for this I was grateful. Any frustrations I may have considered regarding continuing the climb or quitting and going back were quickly absolved when Namche's village rooftops finally came into view.

At last we crossed under the village arch through the usual series of stupas and prayer wheels. Passing 12,200 feet by then, it had gotten chilly outside, but exhilarating. A caravan of mules walked by us and carried their heavy loads up through the village streets. Their Tibetan and Nepali prayer bells were part of the endless enchantment. There was only one way into this place - and that was on foot, and nothing moved up there faster than the speed of yak.

Earlier on the trail, my guide had spun me off the path to where, for a moment, he acted as if we were chasing some noble, profound secret. The direction he took through the brush was someplace I knew not many people had trekked. So I followed him through the grassy path with its overgrowth of vines and branches to a small clearing that overlooked the wide river valley. I thought this is what Hansah wanted me to see and I gazed into the deep gorge from where we stood and admired the view. "Nice Hansah, that's pretty far down there. I don't suppose they base jump any of the cliffs around here, do they?" Half joking, knowing he wouldn't have the slightest idea about hurling off a steep mountainside cliff with a parachute.

"Sah, parachute rides are in next valley near Topie Lapsha. No hikers come to dis spot. Dis is my spot. Dis is where you give me bonus tip. Please look up the valley to our Chomolungma Mountain," he pointed as I obeyed.

Mountain? I questioned, there were mountains all over the place, and I hadn't recognized the Tibetan word for *Everest* that he just used. Nevertheless, I followed his gaze up through the narrow forest ravine. Several miles off, there was a cloud at the top of the saddle that separated the green edge of timberline from the higher, larger scree to the north. It eagerly sat against an everyday

Himalayan backdrop and the dark blue sky. Then, as if under some spontaneous command, the features were ordered to change in the mid-day sun. The cloud slid down off the cone shaped monolith that unveiled what I hadn't expected to see for hours to come – maybe never. But I was taken aback, suddenly peering face-to-face at the tallest, most spectacular peak on earth – *Mount Everest*.

From where we stood on the outcropping of grass, I got my first full glimpse of the crown of the world's highest summit and a surge of pride welled up inside of me. The summit was unmistakable. It soared above everything else in the panorama between me and beyond what I could see, and Hansah had treated me to something others wouldn't get to see for days, maybe never if the weather didn't break for them on the higher peaks.

Jubilant, I looked at him with a nod, thankful for the gift he'd just presented me. Back out on the main trail, we mapped the route we'd take tomorrow to get to an even better spot for a look. We were going to cross over a high airfield outpost to get a more complete mountain view and I was enamored with the prospect. Now that Namche Bazar had been reached, I could relax and take time to enjoy my growing success.

~

Men roam through life for reasons they cannot describe. If a wandering spirit takes hold of their heart, most men don't have the strength enough to ignore it. Sometimes this spirit settles a while, maybe in the arms of a woman. Maybe a warm hearth in a big house gets them to waver another year or two from their quest. But moving forward is still part of the dream. Staying put is the challenge, the question no one can answer unless it's for the love of another. *"I'd stay for her.... if she asked. I'd go if she really wanted...."*

In the previous pages, I mentioned a couple of reasons for coming to Nepal and making this climb. First, was to actually do it and get places higher than I've ever climbed before and not die in the process. And the second was to research a new and controversial book I'd like to write while treading through the risks of its divine speculation and forbidden ground. There were rewards and dangers with both.

But I failed to mention a third. I was escaping my life in the world after surviving a breakup with a woman I loved; someone I never thought would leave my side. But I found I was wrong. I honestly believed she was the last person I would ever devote my soul to. I'd be wrong there as well. Only the future could present me with options that would soothe my aching heart. Though for now I was making this trip without anyone along to see if I could free myself from the chains of that loss. She had me so encased in emotional bondage that sometimes I wondered if I could even breathe without her in my life. She was the inspiration I used to get through my doubt, the wall against my inklings of insecurity. When I was with her she gave me unwavering confidence. When she left our relationship behind for something more important in her life, I had to fight to regain my natural bearing again: one that was strong and motivated to conquer the world if I wanted.

The bottom line was that I loved her - I loved her a lot. And that love went beyond the measures of human possession, although she might have felt like a prisoner from that, so who was I kidding? Maybe she needed to get away from me for a while. Maybe I needed to get away from her. To me, our former attachment was greater than any need one person could have for another. I loved this woman... because I wanted to.

As I dawdled along on the trek, I thought about my life and its less-than-splendid state of affairs. I thought about my ex-wife and how I'd messed her over just the same. People never realize the pain of that crap until the shoe is on the other foot. I watched the streams and tributaries running off the pure mountain snow melt down toward the valley and into the lost, melting-pot of the white, Doot Koshie River. The further I traveled off the beaten path, seeking my own significant 'source' of unity toward an original self, the more faded away from my self-righteous cares I'd become.

It was clear to me how to repair the damage that was done to my spirit, and, if it wasn't too late, maybe I could fix what I had done to others as well.

The revelation of treating everyone with veneration, honesty, and a principle of respect was like the baptism of those crystal waters running their course over rocky, stubborn boulders. I thought about where I was in these mountains, about being spiritually and physically part of something bigger than I could ever hope to be from my past. I realized that when I got back to the world, I would need to be like those streams, running free and natural before they slammed into the milky river and got clouded up in the mix. A new focus was waiting for me if I chose to stay on the path. It might even last if I wasn't absorbed in thinking that I needed total enlightenment for peace. If my insecurities fled on the trails of these great slopes, I could learn to keep them away at home.

I walked along these beautiful trails and thought about Kate. I thought about how easy it could be to add her – *or anyone* – as an infatuation to my life. But is that what I wanted? I had been hurt from a failed love for the last several years, and I knew it was time to move on. Trekking through Nepal renewed my positive, confident perspective, at least for a while. I knew I could dare to be a real person again to someone who mattered. I could reach inside *myself* and accept love back in my life again, maybe find a girl who could enjoy me as well.

B.T. Dormire

View from the lower trail in Namche Bazar. Photo: Byron Dormire.

Namche Bazar was 'fit' into the crux of a mountain bowl, with huts and brick buildings stacked above each other like the curved, terraced seating at the end of a great stadium.

Once inside the village it became apparent that there were hikers making last minute purchases for creature comforts, snivel gear, or personal needs. The mountaineering shops adorned all the name brand equipment from crampons to lip-block. Trekkers were handing over assortments of gear to talented tinkerers to fix or replace broken parts on their rigs, ripped clothing, or bent up trekking poles.

One guy had his sleeping bag gored by a jube-que through the bottom of his pack. Both pieces were torn to shreds and had to be sewn up before he could go on. I figured just before the animal slammed into the hiker it must have thought, *"Get the hell out of the way, you dumb ass - pack train's a comin' through!"* It reminded me that the horns of the jube-ques were sharp and their tempers were short.

Hansah told me over and over, "Stay clear of the pack

trains, Mr. Byron. Always move to the inside line." *Good man,* I thought, as I made a mental note to beef up his tip.

We trekked on up a walkway and skirted dogs rough-housing in the alleys. A cock fight ensued at the fork in the road-bricks ahead with a couple of youngsters tormenting the feisty birds with sticks and pebbles. After a last, gradual rise further into the village, we finally found our lodge for the night, the Namche Hotel.

It didn't look like much from the outside, just a couple of merchants selling nick-knacks or maps, and there was an Eastern religious and modern music vendor that doubled as an internet café. But it is when we walked deeper inside the hotel that we grew more interested at what lay ahead. The cubicles we were shown were clean and efficient. There was a private loo and shower in each and I was relieved that I might be getting a room with a view.

At first glance, Ana Meya Sherpa, the hotel's owner, appeared to be somewhat of a celebrity in her own right. She was a jolly woman with a truly hostess nature about her, joyful in fact. Many people were crowded around her as she was obviously the nucleus of the hotel restaurant and lodge. Her humility was only outdone by the scores of pictures she had on the walls taken of her with all kinds of important people who frequented the special mountain village. There were no less than ten luminaries of state from countries all over the world. These dignitaries, who, of course, were never grandiose about their public relations platforms, were conspicuously tied to the sponsored teams that conquered the Everest range on their country's behalf. Topping the great summits and other 8,000 meter monsters sprinkled throughout Nepal and in neighboring Tibet, had always held the public's interest and general esteem.

In several pictures, Ana Meya was standing with the ambassadors from countries like Korea, Norway, Japan, and the United States. Other mountaineering celebrities were pictured with her as well. Female climbers Edurne Pasaban from Spain, and the Austrian great, Gerlinde Kaltenbrunner both adorned beaming smiles with Ana at their sides. Both women and American Edmund Viesturs were veterans of summiting the world's fourteen highest peaks (8,000 meters), the latter two individuals doing so without any supplemental oxygen.

That night at the lodge, and in a swirl of activity, the dining room quickly filled to capacity. Dozens of hotel guests and probably others from around the village gathered inside the Namche restaurant for chow. To say that things were international here would be a towering understatement. I'd conversed with Russians, Swedes, and Japanese, all of whom were with bigger expeditions heading up to higher summit laurels.

There were East Europeans and Balkan states represented as well. Teams from Romania, Croatia, and Macedonia were all crowded into a separate dining room, lavished with more photos, brass and copper vases, antique teapots and serving ladles. Surprisingly, there were fewer Americans present than I would have thought. Maybe the weakened U.S. economy kept them away, or just a lackluster reluctance to vacation this far away in October when there were so many other places instead.

As the night wore on, I noticed something peculiar; Hansah and Furbar had disappeared. In fact, there wasn't a guide or porter in sight. Nepal has a standing class system where trekkers come first with lodging, food, and even paths on the trail. So the great dining quarters had separate sections for the Nepalese hiking crews. *Too bad;* I thought, I had a jillion questions about the ornaments and ancient artifacts on the shelves behind my seat. Hansah was great at giving me historical overviews and the waitresses were too busy to stop and chat about things they've probably answered a thousand times in the past.

It wasn't long before the food arrived and after that, bedlam was the order of the night. I always braved the boiled potatoes and mixed vegetables, and in this place, it was some of the better food I'd eaten on the entire trip. Protein still came from the Snickers bars and vitamin supplements, but an occasional bowl full of the protein-rich dal baht waft by and you could hear the chants and chuckles coming from the Sherpa's room as they joked, "Dal baht power, 24-hour!" Meaning, I assumed, that if you could get through the clay taste of lentil, you were good to go for a while.

The restaurant staff started bringing in plates of chicken balls and noodles, one after the next. Rolls were tossed around like baseballs from one end of the grand serving tables to the other and everyone was having a great time. Most of them were going higher from here, lunging to places with peaks of 18,000 feet or more.

Finishing off a tall Carlsberg at altitudes above 12,000 feet probably blurred my vision more than I would have liked. To relish a freezing, upcoming shower and an otherwise critter-ridden, overused bunk, I might not have seemed so eager if I wasn't inebriated *and* heading for another early morning rise.

But before I could get to my feet and bid the Norwegians goodnight, Katie Summers walked through the main entry doors with her Australian contingent and looked straight at me from across the crowded room. She motioned me over to her table like there was not going to be any argument about it, and that was that.

Damn! It was going to be another two hours before I headed for bed. We sat through her dinner and shared several glasses of rum. We fed each other portions of a great apple desert and inwardly I imagined accompanying her for several stages of the rest of our lives. She laughed when I told her about how ripped my thighs felt from climbing those last couple of miles. We agreed that Nepal was magni-ficent, that the mosaic of switchbacks we had just separately scaled fell neatly against the backdrop of the rolling Himalayan landscape. Getting to Namche was just part of our reward for making the trip. Meeting each other again in this faraway place, *I thought to myself*, was another.

My legs stayed permanently cramped while we talked and I secretly hoped they would last the next few days trudging up and down the never-ending slopes. Kate and I eventually bid farewell for the night. I think both of us believed that a certain comfort level had transpired while we bonded together as friends. I knew I'd see her again somewhere. Silently, we both wondered how to make the long distance between our countries work if we gave it a try.

As a final joke to my senses, I almost flipped when the inn keeper led me down the hallway and pointed up to my room. In all the night's lore I had forgotten where I was at. I couldn't believe what I was seeing, but sure enough, there it was: to get to my bedroom, I was going to have to climb *another* flight of stairs before the end of my night.

❧

The Views and Some Tea

Day 5 - 11 October, 2012

Thursday morning and we had a terribly early wake-up. It was 4:40 and I was tired, hungry, and cold. I met Hansah at 5:00 so he could guide me up to a Buddhist monastery overlooking the Syangboche panorama.

Darting through the lodge entrance and out the front gates, we set out to the upper west side of Namche village. We planned to hike the easier trail up past the Zarok hut cluster and across the high plateau of Syangboche's dirt airstrip. I felt enticed looking at the rising path before me, energized by recalling yesterday's pitch straight up from Monjo. I took this next leg in the climb as a sign that I might actually reach my goal – bragging rights as a fledgling Himalayan trekker, finding the one great place in these mountains to stand and take in a rich Everest view.

When a person hikes or walks anyplace special, there are two states of occupation that go through their mind. First, they concentrate on watching their step, one step at a time, especially if it's a haggard, bumpy trail. It's how a Zen pupil keeps from lapsing into thinking about anything other than one foot in front of the other, step after step, mile after mile.

Second, and for the rest of us, focusing our steps on a trailhead is simply a prelude to the self-centered thinking we always revert to once we've begun. Oh, we watch where we're going at first, just like everybody else. But then a process takes shape and we slide into solving the world's problems during our stroll - *or solving our own.* This second activity is how we drift into thought about something specific. It's a move that takes us from the introspection of Zen practice and the ultimate *no-thought* experience, to a more venerable state of existentialism which may be just the opposite - *I, I, I, me, me, me! Did you see that adventurous thing I just did?* Or, even more distasteful, *Look, I've achieved something great here, now gimme' this, that, or whatever in return.*

Trekking, or tootling along like this as one might enjoy, can result in a more refined clarity toward understanding experiential observation. When a person enters one or both of these two states, they evolve into someone more capable of genuine levity, specific intent, or forthright affection.

As I walked through the pre-dawn darkness above Namche Bazar, I had to laugh about dinner the night before. There was a rowdy group of British trekkers, wealthy day-hikers most likely, who were extremely fit and seemed to compete with each other over whose recipe could improve the dry, lentil flavored *dal baht* more. The women figured that fresh vegetables and plenty of greens along with their idea of a secret spice or two would hit the spot. Problem up there was that you couldn't find enough of any of the right spices and ingredients to make a hearty, fulfilling meal.

The men believed that marinated, gourmet selections of beef chunks or ham would do the trick. But seeing as how both of the men's delicacies were sensitive culinary subjects in this part of the world, there'd be nothing doing with that either. The consensus finally arrived when one of them suggested splashing rum, pepper, and cinnamon over a bowl of the large, square noodles and by the time you finished eating them, you'd be too pissed to care!

That got a rise out of everyone's beer for a toast. "Too pissed to care!" they all said as a team, clanking their glasses and adding more laughs. They blurted a few British, *'Here-here's',* and back-slapped other patrons in their corner of the dining area that was enlivened and chatty.

The German expedition was at first, more solemn than the boisterous Norwegians who sat next to me and automatically launched into ribaldry as soon as they entered the room. Even the stoic Koreans across the table eventually loosened up after a few shots of the Nepalese raxi. Remembering this potent liquor's ability to sneak up on people, especially at the altitudes we were sitting, I knew what was coming next from the Bavarian climbers. It only took one joke from the German team's cinematographer to explode the Rhineland's finest into jovial songs and knocking each other around.

Smiling, I remembered how the Australian contingent lumbered into the hotel restaurant and I saw Kate staring back at me from the door. When she glared in and pointed straight at me to get over to her table I knew that was it for my night. Once more I had found myself in her company and I felt really good about it. I couldn't help but reflect that I'd set a pattern for myself on this trip. My vacation days up on the trail resembled a more resplendent combination of flirts, work, and play than I have when I'm actually on a job back home, *flirting*, *working*, or *playing*. Everyone in that room had busted their asses getting to and from these mountain hideaways. It was work! And because most of them were experts at letting off steam, there wasn't a somber face in the crowd, so it was one helluva a party as well.

I hoped that the 10,000-kilometer sojourn I was on between Colorado, Kabul's highlands in Afghanistan, and our restaurant gathering at the Namche Hotel, would be rewarded with an inspiring view of the great mountain on everyone's list - *Sagarmatha Chomolungma*, Mount Everest. Of course, the region where I was having dinner that night, with all its majesty and splendor, was a place that shadowed the rest of the earth from there. After my Carlsbergs and the elation of conversations with Kate, I assumed I had made it to heaven, or at least from my personal approach to wishful thinking, a good portion of the way up the route.

The path looming ahead of us at 5:20 a.m. was just coming into perspective as the pre-dawn light was breaking over the mountainous silhouettes. We were in for a 1,200-foot vertical ascent that would ease us past the Khumjung Hillary School, and the Tenzing Norgye memorial. Still too early for any respectable illumination, the government yak farm was an interesting surprise. A lone Sherpa ranch hand was casting hay and grass in large, steamy clumps out of a donkey-drawn cart for the dozen or so yaks milling about like furry statues, frozen in the morning chill. They didn't seem to be in any hurry to plod over and mow down the feed as the frustrated rancher tried to coax them to eat.

Hansah and I had a goal. We were to scramble up to see Mount Everest before the morning clouds rolled in and obscured any possible view. Within the growing heights and thinning air before us, the trail we took to the Everest viewpoint was much easier than the route the other tourists tried later that morning. Ours was a mild, vigorous climb with grazing jube-ques untethered in different spots along the rise. The tourist's pitch would be daunting, straight up over loose, slippery shale. Its rocky terrain and steep, nasty switchbacks lay in an almost chaparral-like, San Gabriel-type mountain landscape. It was going to be dusty and tough for them.

Team Shizen was the first that morning to trek above Namche Bazar and well past the edge of timberline into the Himalayan tundra. Hansah was again taking me to the best viewpoint this side of the higher locations still miles from where we stood. Moving along the upper plateau, a perfectly clear view of Everest and Lhotse peaks emerged from the early dawn. I was observably humbled, standing there and staring at the full rim of the mountainous peaks which horseshoed a valley that had taken a hundred-million years to form. Life has been generous to me so far, but I never expected a view like this.

We moved on across the flat toward a small shrine at the

edge of the trail. There was a fresh crematory of stones next to the stupa that sat by itself there in the grassy field. Apparently the night before we stumbled upon it, someone was cremated by their family and sent to the heavens. The rocks were scorched in different places, but there was no smell or any other visual evidence of remains. It was a peaceful area in a green, rolling meadow, and there'd be good shade from the small mimosas growing under the shadows of the Everest range. All the other peaks that rimmed the valley walls were like ancient thrones the deceased could call their final resting grounds.

After what seemed like a moment of silence between Hansah and me, we figured it was time to go get some breakfast. He reminded me that I was paying for the meal, but in looking around from the plateau, I couldn't yet tell where we were heading. With a small degree of mischief, he pointed off to an image in the trees about a quarter-mile across from where we stood. To my surprise, the breakfast nook to which he referred was the famed Everest View Hotel. So, in wasting no time, we clamored back down a small hillside glade of juniper pines to the hotel grounds sitting at 13,300 feet.

We entered the main entrance where the wood and brick cornices were trimmed to perfect angles, and trundled right through the main lobby toward the glass-lined restaurant. Before realizing if we could even eat there, Hansah and I plopped ourselves down on an outside table overlooking a spectacular view. From the balcony where we were seated, I got my best close-up pictures of Everest and the surrounding range. I thought to myself, *This _must_ be where God comes to sit and relax.*

The hotel was Japanese built and very posh. I ordered an omelet again, dried fruits, and some toast, only because I figured this was a solid staple for my system that I could depend on until I got back to the world. I'd been nursing my gurgling stomach over the last few days, but not as bad as the stop I needed on the switchbacks between Monjo and Namche Bazar. As the sun crested the first ridges to the north and west, the big peaks started forming clearer images into view. Lhotse, Chomolungma (*Tibet's name for Everest*), and the great precipice, Ama Dablam, to name a few; they were each sitting cloud-free in that early morning air.

The presence of Cho Oyu and other 8,000-meter peaks slipping up from the Tibetan (*Chinese*) side of the Everest wall could be felt more than seen, but the tips of their summits were visible from the Syangboche plateau nevertheless. I was surrounded by magnificence. And as far as I could tell, this was where that word was invented. Some lonely wanderer stumbled into these ramparts and looking up from his trek, murmured to no one but himself. "Magnificent!" he would have proclaimed, and he would have meant every syllable.

Mount Everest, left. Lhotse Peak, right. Photo by Byron Dormire.

Sitting there, I felt what must have been the same emotion, reveling in the geographic majesty of the mountains around me. I loved the physical and spiritual exhilaration I gained from plodding along this new and challenging path. Oh, I could sit in a teahouse reflecting on the aches and pains of my day. Or I could lean in silence against a stone retaining wall next to a Sherpa on a break. Between his towering load and my penchant to whine about the most trivial discomfort, both of us would measure instead, the appreciation we held for something bigger than ourselves. I was ardently aware of the humility and pitfalls I now faced in my life - that I was nothing compared to the existence of everything else.

After my fleeting glimpses of *Chomolungma* from overlooks stolen between side paths and tree lines, I finally got my bucket list fulfilled. I sat before the towering crown of Mount Everest and was very lucky (according to Hansah) that the weather had been unrivaled on our trip and was cooperating just fine.

I finished my jam and toast on the veranda of the Everest View overlook. It was something I could have done dressed in my pajamas as much as anything else, but I sat back and admitted that I couldn't think of a more incredible place in the world to have a morning breakfast. And I'd be absolutely right.

Many hikers eclipsed me this climbing season and had conquered these slopes as old as their sixties and seventies. Some passed me in the lowlands even older and fitter than I had imagined. For the most part, they were all heading to Everest's base camp. I climbed that morning from the Namche Hotel sitting at levels between 11,740 feet and 12,200, to the highest resort in the world - The Everest View', at 13,085 feet. For me, that was the extent of my high altitude jaunt. For everyone else with more time and money on their hands than dirt, it was only a taste of what they had left to explore.

My guide and I plodded back down to Namche about 9:00 a.m., but not before a family of hotel guests were rushing around in a panic trying to get off the mountain as fast as they could. Apparently the teenage son of a couple from Birmingham was suffering under the effects of HACE and had to get back to a lower spot off the mountain before something more serious took effect. Hansah and I watched the frantic parents scurry to get their lodgings paid for and get on the trail toward the depths of Lukla below. "Too bad," he said to me. "People climb too fast. They ruin their stay."

"Yeah, Hansah, too bad," I said, looking over at him like I was glad it wasn't me. He shook his head with a growing smile, like, *Ah-huh, we're lucky it wasn't you either.* I couldn't help but think I had climbed too fast myself. Between yesterday's assault out of Monjo and this little pitch for fruit juices and breakfast that overlooked Tengboche and the Chhatyang river valley, I didn't think I was in that big a hurry. I asked him, "Is there any kind of cure for people who get that condition, other than going back down in altitude?"

He said, "Yes. You need the Nepali system again. This time, you must collect the milk of a mountain tiger, and then drink every bit of it while you run downhill from the tiger and not spill a drop. That way you don't worry about headaches anymore, only the tiger. Thank you very much, sah."

Of course, and why not? How silly of me. All one had to do was simply collect the milk of a mother tiger and, no more headaches. I kind of saw his point.

We left sight of the EV Hotel and descended the long hilly slope that preceded the eastern switchbacks over Namche Village. I was satisfied with the great views we got of the big mountains though a bit jealous of the trekkers heading further up the trail to points closer than I would ever get on this trip. In a few days we would be at the end of this amazing journey. There were two more overnight stops to go before we got off the mountain and we still had a lot of work ahead. Though I struggled in some places with my breathing and muscle fatigue on the uphill swings, my health remained intact.

Just as we entered the upper end of the meadow grasses, I came upon my first good look at a giant yak, up close and personal. We definitely surprised each other as I rounded the path. He was standing there chewing on thick grassy clumps and looking at me as I stopped and stared right back. This yak was big and healthy with a clean brown and silver coat, and he had the typically hairy underbelly, hooves, and tail. I tried getting a picture next to him but my guide couldn't get the shot to save his life. So here I was chasing this 600-pound pack animal around through the shrubs and thistle hoping for a smile. I almost got my ass gored when it turned on us and grunted some sort of yak-style *get lost, you idiots*. Hansah and I got the message and we trotted on down the path laughing about it, but leaving the beast to itself just the same.

Dropping through the arduous switchbacks was going to be easy compared to the climbs, but that still didn't take away from the difficulties I had with my knees and joints. Weight distribution is much harder on the extremities when a hiker pounds along the burdening slopes. Rocky, uneven blocks of root-crossed steps; steep, rutted out furrows and crags in the powdery sand; slippery bouts with piss-filled mud on the path from jube-que and pack-mule waste all played havoc on controlling my stride.

We scaled down a more difficult route than the one we climbed. It slung us past the lower east side of the Syangboche dirt airstrip then dropped straight down a series of steep, dirty turns with huge stone stairways that did absolutely nothing for my knees, hips, and ankles. The unkempt runway had jube-ques grazing on the short tundra grass, and I couldn't see landing anything on it other than maybe one of those Russian heavy resupply choppers, or a Pelotas Porter short-field aircraft. I imagined the Porter weaving in on a low-pass to scatter the animals off the runway stretch. Then again, I could see the listless jube-ques standing wherever they wanted and ignoring the plane swooping in from above. Probably not a big deal for either; the Porter could land on a dime and the helicopter wouldn't think twice.

From here, we advanced to a point where the day-overs were heading up past us to the EV Hotel for brunch. These were the trekkers who were staying in Namche an extra period of time to acclimatize for their further destinations up the pass. *Kate wasn't among them.* When it was all said and done, most of them were aiming for Everest's base camp, and the steep jaunt up the east side of Namche was sure to give them a taste of the climbing to come. To me, many of these folks didn't appear to be able to make a lap around the inside of a mall, let along tackle the rigors of heading through 5,000 meter passes and on up to the tops of 18,000 foot peaks just for a view of the monster.

But who was I to judge these dreamers? I imagined myself up there too. Though I wasn't in the peak of fitness, I was in better shape than most. And though I climbed the easier route that morning before the sun came up, I still thought I was going to die from the effort; I felt their pain. The more time I spent higher up on the trail, the slower I plodded along. The trade off, of course, was that I worked less because of it and could watch my pace. I learned about pacing by climbing peaks in the Rockies. There you had to watch the clock and obey the adage, 'summit by noon, be off by two'. High mountain areas can make their own weather, namely storms, and they frequently do so, especially in summer. It's imperative to avoid the lightning that plagues mountaineers in that part of the world. I wasn't sure how things fared in the Himalayas.

My lungs held out for most of the day, but the descent was a total fiasco on all my bones, muscles, and other extremities – *even my hair hurt* – and I wasn't even carrying any weight. I talked with a few of the hikers on their ascent, reassuring them that the top of the pretty plateau wasn't far off. Everyone on a descent always lies through their teeth about that, "Oh, it's just up the rise. You're almost there. You can do it. Good job!"

This was a Himalayan mountain range - you're *never* almost there!

Hansah and I finally made it to the bottom of the Namche slope and as luck would have it, we ran smack dab into a yak pack which added to the true Himalayan feel of the hike.

A small Sherpa girl herded the yaks down the narrow cobblestone walk, yelling her enchanting calls and moving them along. The yaks were slow and deliberate as they walked, their bells clanging and jingling a lot like a horse-drawn carriage clomping through Central Park on a lone, snowy night. It seemed that the big bells hung off the more senior yaks to guide the younger ones trailing in from behind. They could also be ringing to warn us to clear the trail, a more practical explanation most hikers would accept. But naturally, a third, enlightening purpose must have included greeting the spirits for luck and good health. The wide, unblinking eyes of each wary animal stared into me as the girl yelped and kindly swatted them forward with her rope, reading my mind, smiling at me as she passed *"Namaste, Mr. Hiker."*

"Namaste, Sweetie." It was almost like the beasts were as curious about me standing there for no apparent reason, as I was about them walking by. They trod along and obeyed the chants and taunts of their master on another mindless day.

They were gorgeous.

At the bottom of the slope, but not quite to the edge of Namche's upper-east end, there was a fork in the path that led past the village school yard that doubled as the Nepalese army post. From the top of my hike near the airstrip and then all the way down, I had watched the morning's callisthenics and company formations, and later on, the kids out playing in the open parade field. When we got there, we took the fork to the left away from the village and wound up in a plush meadow with another promising view of the Everest valley and its peaks.

The Sagarmatha National Park Headquarters office was up there and someone said this wasn't as good a view as up the slope at the hotel, but I was just as pleased with how beautiful the peaks appeared from where we sat on the grass. In fact, I was so content that I laid back and fell asleep right there on the meadow grounds in the warm Himalayan sun, basking in the satisfaction that I was still in Nepal and breathing their rarefied, pure mountain air.

I probably wasn't asleep more than ten or fifteen minutes, but it recharged my engines and I was eager to plop down the rest of the hill and get back to my room. We checked out of the hotel about

12:30 and started back toward Phakding and Lukla. Before I got to the village limits, I heard my name being called through the crowds we passed swarming the alley shops. "Byron! Hey, back here." I turned around and noticed that everyone had looked up and stared at the beautiful woman calling my name, walking toward me with a bounce. I felt like I'd just been recognized amidst a crowd of movie stars by the prettiest girl at the ball; as if all their money and clout didn't amount to squat because I was the focus of her dreams.

Sure enough, Kate had seen me and my guys trudging by one of the gear outlets and she came breezing out to stop my escape. "Were you going to leave today without saying goodbye?" she asked, seeming a little crestfallen that I would do such a thing.

"Ah, no, Kate, I wasn't. I thought you were with the rest of the swarm from last night doing a little sightseeing at the monasteries up in Phungi Thanga," I said. "Now I'm glad to see that you didn't go."

She smiled and looked anxious about something; like she was relieved she caught me before I was gone. She said, "I knew you were hiking up the hill this morning and I wanted to wish you a safe trip home. I really enjoyed our dinner last night and I was hoping we could meet online and talk again in the future."

I was elated that she caught me when she did. I was getting that awkward sensation that I better say something profound, or just forget the whole thing right then and there. "Kate, I figured if you wanted to keep in contact you'd have given me your email already. But since you didn't, I thought you were good with the time we shared and that was it. I didn't want to push any more than I already had."

"Byron, I didn't think you wanted to make contact anymore, or were just kidding about it before, so I didn't say anything either."

Hansah and Furbar were used to this by now and were snickering at me from further down the walk. Okay then, fine. I decided to come right out with it. "All right Kate, may I please have your email address so we can joke about how silly you looked last night with a Nepalese party hat on after three glasses of rum?"

"I thought you'd never ask," she said and she pulled a neatly folded paper from her parka and handed it over. I opened it briefly and saw that she'd written a couple of paragraphs atop the contact info. She pushed my hands down and aside and turned a cute, beat red. "Don't read that here," she said. "Wait till you get down the hill. If you still want to write after that, then I'll be waiting for you to remember how to type."

All of the sudden my world seemed less volatile than it had just minutes before. We were heading in opposite directions that day, two separate people who were light years apart, but as we grasped each other's arms to say goodbye I was thinking that I hadn't felt that enchanted with a woman in a long, long time. After that brief little soiree, the going varied with me for the rest of the trip. There were steep descents that pounded my body, and grudgingly merciless trails leading up and down each neighboring valley, taking so much of my breath that I almost passed out from the effort, but none of that mattered anymore. After seeing Kate one last time traipsing out of that mountain gear outlet, my aches and pains on this trek were the farthest thing from my mind.

~

We made it to Monjo again and stopped in at the same little place we stayed a couple of nights back, the Namaste Guest House. The plan was sketched out to make it to Phakding a bit further down the trail. We'd wake in the morning from there and tromp a final uninterrupted blitz into Lukla. We'd banked on getting there early enough to get a room before the big crowds hit. If we didn't arrive before they filled all the quarters - either coming or going, we'd have to settle for a tent in some field instead. There was another possibility, even if things worked out with a room at Furbar's place in Lukla, we would not be put off if there happened to be a quick flight back into to Kat'.

However, that plan was on hold. At the request of the 'Guest House owners, Thao and Sophie, *Team Shizen* was welcomed again with open arms and we were ushered straight to our previous rooms. I shrugged as we were enthusiastically taken in, much to the chagrin, I suspect, of the other patrons quietly waiting to register in the main dining foyer. (My $20 tip from two days before probably didn't hurt). Thao already had my room with the riverside view warmed up and ready and I couldn't carry my bags for a song. After settling in, I came back to the dining area to sit for a while writing in my journal and to read Katie's note:

> *Dear Sir Edmund, (Byron),*
>
> *I came on this vacation to get away from work and the everyday routine of my unpretentious life back in Longreach, (Queensland). I guess like everybody else up here, I just wanted to find a little more of myself along the way; or at least someone I could recognize as such when I finally returned to my home. But as chance would have it, we crossed paths at the airport and now, I keep bumping into you on the trail. There is something different about you, Byron, and I can't help but think that this is anything other than some grand, mystical coincidence set in motion to mess with our brains. But you bring a smile to my face.*
>
> *That said, I believe things happen for a reason. If for no other purpose than we were meant to be friends into a long and pleasant future, then I'd say my trip is already worth it. I'm glad we got to visit for a few minutes over dinner. If, in your worldly travels you happen to remember who wrote you this note, drop me a line sometime and maybe I'll tease you from down under. (:-)*
>
> *You're an interesting person, Mr. America, and you make me laugh. Safe travels for the rest of your stay.*
>
> *Kate Summers*
Email enclosed.

Indeed, I thought to myself as I sat there and sipped the hot chai Sophie brought in for me unannounced. That this was a very nice letter from a very nice girl. What the hell was I going to do with a beautiful woman who lived 7,000 miles away from the States?

Back to reality. Inside at the Namaste Guest House, I was asked to eat with the family in the privacy-kitchen which was obviously a well-respected honor, and I was set nearest the heat from the wood-burning stove. I took a turn rocking the baby in his homemade wicker crib. He was now twenty-six days old - *two more than our previous visit, duh!* and I smiled watching Thao and his wife cooking and making merriment between each other over the evening's dinner. I could hear the other guests in the dining room outside the curtain loosening up with laughs and reminisces about the day's events. Sophie enlisted Hansah to start taking their orders and serving up meals.

This second night's crowd in Monjo was an eclectic bunch. There was a strong blonde couple from Canada, some youth group from Austria bundled under a yak-wool blanket along the benches near the window, and a trio of Israeli students I'd passed back and forth all day on the trail. I heard that Sherpas don't cotton to trekkers from Israel because they complain too much and are skimpy with tips. But these three were easy-going and, as I later learned, they had hiked the inland route which takes a good two weeks from the outskirts of Kathmandu. I thought that was pretty ambitious of them, but I suppose if one had the time, then why not?

After dinner and as darkness fell outside the lodge, the three young hikers brewed up a special blend of 'mountain coffee' and passed it around to the guests. I wondered if I was just being naïve or trying to be funny, but when they handed me my cup I had to ask if it wasn't laced with some form of spiritual hashish or other fanciful herb.

As I clearly recalled, it was their response in unison that brought a cheerful new atmosphere to the lodge. They briskly replied to all of us who stopped and glanced at them for an answer, "Why...yes, *Yes, it is!"*

Oh boy, I thought to myself, wondering how I was going to get out of this one. "Can you guys brew up a straight batch for me? I can't do the other stuff (*anymore*), but a cup of tea sounds great about now." They easily complied, boiling it up on their little Nova camp stove, and I settled in and enjoyed an abundance of their hot, mango tea. And then I relegated myself to overdose on coconut biscuits from Thao's concessions display. I'd wave or nod like I was some kind of auction-goer at Sotheby's in England and the cookies would just keep on coming.

As I had already found amid the culture of these explorers, adventure-trekkers, and Sherpas alike, discussions at night were vibrant and entertaining. I learned about some of the monasteries and villages higher up the route. The older, grander of which may have entertained a lone, interesting visitor two-thousand years back. Could Jesus *(Issa)* have in fact, walked these lands, I wondered? I revisited that theory from time to time along my trip, quietly wondering if he had crossed these same paths, seen the same majestic peaks I gazed upon just a day or two before, or laughed with these joyful, spiritual people as I had laughed, with warmth in my heart.

I was certainly intrigued by the local's interpretation of mountain superstitions, and how the spirits watch over and protect the penitent hikers on the trail. I wondered if I'd been respectful enough to be included in that special group.

I was pleased yet again that I only had myself to content with as the evening came to an end. Even if there was a bit of residual *'student coffee'* awash in my tea, that was a night that I slept like a rock.

☯

Part III: Prayers of the Monkey God

Pride suddenly blazed up inside him. He was no longer a shramana, it was no longer appropriate for him to beg. He gave the rice cake to a dog and remained without food.

Siddhartha, *Hermann Hesse.*

Festivals enliven the soul. Ceremony enriches it. The Nepalese people are tolerant, happy, and inspiring. Within their religious and cultural synergy, anyone who ventures into this land will find a people prospering from the harmonious obligations set forth by God. They will see people of all ages - teenagers side-by-side with the elderly - living daily acts of worship and rituals, respecting the particular deities they seek for their needs, and loving the duty they have accepted with their cross-generational friendships, relationships, and the honors they bestow on their ancestors near and far.

This solitary, stress-free life is sought by many. When hiking into realms above 12,000 feet, one often asks, can I find myself at peace up here while the world below me is in tears?

Is there an ultimate goal of the trekker? Can one hike to find an increase in love? Can people venture to unknown lands to locate simplicity in their lives? Or, is experiencing spiritual unity among life's ecological and geographical harmonies the ultimate answer instead? Something you could find in your own backyard instead of some venture a million miles away?

People hike for personal reasons, either physical or emotional in nature. But all of us keep moving up or down, going forward or back. We're always in a cycle of change that never ends.

☯

Escaping Mother Earth

Day 6 - October 12, 2012

The river's voice nudged me into daylight as it did two mornings before. I'd awakened from dreams of thunder in the faraway valleys, a rumbling, rolling crash that lasted for what seemed to be nearly a minute. But as I slid more into consciousness and stirred under the thick, winter-like covers, the river flowed noisier in my ears and through my head. I realized that I was still in an earthly land far apart from the rest of my otherwise, comfortable, pampered extremes.

Team Shizen was up, packed, and at breakfast once again by 7:00 a.m. I waited for Thao's breakfast special, the morning omelet, and then settled into my journal to top off some notes. The talk and camaraderie between me, my guide, our porter, and the send-off we got from the lodge owners, Thao and Sophie, were almost like we were part of one big family. They were grateful that we came by their lodge again and before we departed, they adorned us with prayer scarves, little reed baskets of caramelized sugar crystals, sweet baked goodies, and juices from their shelf and cabinet supply. Were we supposed to carry all this, I wondered?

It wasn't long before Hansah had each basket tied off with a scarf to the end of some sticks he fashioned from an amba tree and magnolia branches. We looked like a gallivanting misfit of boys from a Huck Finn novel; the only missing indulgence was not tooling off in our bare feet under straw hats and chewing on willow reeds or blackberry brambles.

The walk out of Monjo that morning started at the base of the lower switchbacks and lead back to the river. It was another variety of up and downhill treks as it descended toward Lukla's lower plateau and the final leg of our trip. Dropping out of Namche Bazar like we did, we had originally aimed for Phakding, wanting to pass quickly through Thadokrine to finally crest the last stone stairway for home. When we paused by the Namaste Guest House to say hello and have a quick cup of tea, Sophie was insistent that we stay there again for the night and the rest of our afternoon and evening was a mix of revelry, affection, and envy.

One of the guests I got to know more at breakfast that morning was a fellow from Australia named Michael Rix. He was on his 5th visit to Nepal and journeying this time en route to two high-country challenges. He was heading for the Kala Patthar overlook of Everest's base camp valley, then back through the Kongma La Pass at 18,000-plus feet, and finally around through the Chhukhung village stopover to climb the relatively quirky slopes of Island Peak, towering at a respectable 21,235 feet. He was sixty-three years old. I was inspired by his tenacity and got his email to write him later and hear of his success.

I filmed him bounding up the stone stairway ahead of the jube-ques ambling up the path from below. "Cheers mate. I don't want to get behind those smelly beasts. Drop me a note sometime." And he disappeared over the rise to go live his dreams. Rix was making life happen at 20,000 feet; I was having trouble on the anthills.

The sights we encountered on the return leg of the trek included many of the same wonders we saw on the journey up. There were the overhanging forests, glacial mountain views, animal pack trains, trekkers, porters, and village women beating laundry near their wells. There were also contrasts like the farmer we passed plowing his barley field with a pair of water buffalo on the terrace of a thousand-foot cliff. And we joined a wedding party for a while, parading between villages that praised and encouraged a young bride and groom wearing traditional ceremonial attire. Nepalese traditions were filled with celebration and brightly colored dress.

~

The weather had held out for every leg of the downhill journey, but the wind blew in eerie gusts around the tops of the trees without making a sound on the path below. Offhandedly, I remember the same conditions on the morning of the Los Angeles earthquake in February, 1981. I hadn't thought about earthquakes for years, but now all of the sudden I began to look above me into the steep jagged mountains and wonder if something wasn't brewing up there that we needed to know.

I had looked up a few stories online before the trip and noted a recently published article about the Chaurikharka tremor on August 14th, 2011. A sharp quake loosened up the side of a rocky cliff and five people were killed in a subsequent landslide near Lukla that took one family's house and ripped it completely off the map. Three children and two women died while seeking shelter from the monsoons. They were in a rented house just off the trail close to the Thalsharoa Monastery nestled under a million-year-old shelf of solid rock. This village had stood for ages without so much as a pebble rolling off the face above it. Then, as natural as the eroding forces of nature can be, freezing, jittery elements combined and loosened a truck-size boulder that pummeled down the mountain slope. Tons of scree and talus exploded away from the face in its wake. Anything caught in its path was swept up in the river of rock and debris and never seen or heard from again.

The rumbling I imagined when I woke up earlier, and the small quake I experienced a few days before, were the simmering ingredients for a maelstrom of catastrophe. Mother Earth was waiting to tear down the mountain and cover everything in a broadening swath of destruction no one could stop. We had plopped into a teahouse for hot drinks and snacks just south of a span bridge overlooking the Thado Koshi Khola (mountain stream runoff); its green and crystal clear waters flowed in a rolling torrent down a narrow rocky gorge.

The path leveled out onto a nice flat stretch at the village of Thado Koshigoan and gave us a picture-perfect sightline across the river's expanse to the snow capped, 21,000-foot, Kusum Khangkaru summit. This particular valley was notorious for its ferocity of avalanches and rock slide activity, and *Team Shizen* was about to be introduced to the full force of its unmistakable hello. Dozens of tributaries and waterfalls badgered the steep mountain sides from a constant glacial runoff pouring into the Doot Koshi River below. These mountains were alive and to assume otherwise and not be ready to dive for the closest cover was to laugh in the face of peril.

I had just paid the serving girl for the tea as we started out on the trail to the south. She was standing in the door of the lodge as we walked away and was watching us with her haunting, melancholy eyes, likely wondering what sort of worlds we were part of outside her own beautiful, mountainous prison.

We hadn't gone but a few steps when I felt the first sudden jolt. The ground under us shook with a growing crescendo and rumbling noise that rose above everything else we could hear. Hansah felt that one for sure as he crouched down and covered his head in surprise. I just stood there and balanced on a pair of wobbly legs. The rolling quake swerved the earth beneath us for nearly a minute, dropping at times like plopping a china cabinet down a set of stairs. The roar of what I thought might be its echo followed an instant after it stopped.

Suddenly, a large, exploding crash came next as I heard the movement of tons of broken earth coming at us from high above the teahouse in the trees. Hansah and I both glanced up the slope to determine what our senses hadn't figured out yet in the seconds we had left. We were about thirty feet away from the girl and I could see her face turn to gaping fear as she registered that the whole mountainside was coming down in a fury of earth and rocks and trees.

She scrambled in a panic across the path to the up-slope side of the trail. Ducking under a section of retaining wall, she lay as close to the ground as she could, covering her head and hiding her face. I looked at Hansah for an out, dumbstruck in the instant and wondering if I could get away from this monster before being swept off the edge of the trail and killed.

"POIHIRO!!!" he screamed, (*Landslide!*). He frantically pointed to get against the wall and was already heading there himself. I was getting my legs into action and following suit. Before I dove for the shelter and braced myself against the wall, I looked up and saw what was coming. Tons of rocks, dirt, and snow were crashing toward us like a giant wave obliterating a beach-side sandcastle, and nothing could stop the landslide from swallowing everything that it passed.

I was familiar with a practice we called *bunker diving* from four years of dodging mortars in Iraq. When the rockets started into an area covering about a hundred-square acres, the Counter Rocket, Artillery, and Mortar alarm for that sector would blare into life. The *C-RAM*, as it's affectionately known to folks running for their lives, became a godsend to me in the hostile regions of the world. The troublemakers who live there are the *not-so-friendly-bunch-of-assholes* who try killing coalition members every day. So we have to know where to run and dive for cover in the blink of an eye. If the radar tracks have munitions heading inside a danger-close umbrella, another more startling siren will wail. "Incoming, incoming!" which of course, sends people into a panic and they know there are only seconds to react before a rainstorm of terror pours down and explodes on their heads.

The girl was well versed in the drills of surviving a rock slide. I too actually bounced against the stone retaining wall in a parallel-prone position at the very instant the onslaught of debris careened over our heads and continued down the other side of the trail's edge. The thundering noise behind the landslide quickly settled and left us dusted and covered under a pile of rubble.

I took a cursory inventory of the fact that one, I was still alive, and two, I couldn't feel anything broken or painful enough on my body that I wouldn't recover from in a pinch. I shook the soot off my head and began to look around to see if everyone was okay. Hansah had lurched himself out from under a mix of tree branches and rock and was scurrying over to pull me out and brush me off. A black, silk-furred dog had run over from a neighboring lodge and began barking at a pile of debris where the girl had ducked into just seconds before. We saw a small, dusty arm push through some of the stones and clumps of ferns and pet the dog as it wagged and sniffed and looked over at us like, *Well dumbasses, get your butts over here. I can't get her out by myself!*

Landslide aftermath, cleanup near trail to Lukla. Photo: B.T. Dormire

We quickly found that sixteen-year-old Jasminka Timor had been rolled up in a debris pile and was gasping for air. Hansah and I plunged into the dirt and began ripping at the stones and tree branches that had her trapped underneath. I finally reached through a hole in the rubble and grasped onto what felt like a down vest, then with one fearsome tug I yanked her out of the tiny runoff gully she'd wedged herself into next to the wall. Though she was out and stumbled around, I was holding her steady as she bent over choking and cleaning the dirt from her mouth and nostrils. In between her gagging and hacks, she looked up at Hansah then back over at me and we all started laughing - and crying - together while we dusted each other off. There were porters running down off the trail and villagers coming in from a neighboring field. The dog was barking and yelping in what seemed like a joyful relief.

For the most part, the *poihiro* missed hitting the teahouse with the bulk of the slide. Only a ton of dirt and rocks had settled against the front of the lodge and could be easily cleaned through in a couple of days. The majority of boulders and pines that charged by us continued on down the mountainside to the Doot Koshi. We all lucked out that after-noon and as the neighbors started showing up to assess the damage. They were soon wailing prayers that the gods had protected Jasminka, Hansah, and me, and we were being prodded at to stay for dinner and gifts. There was only one problem we hadn't considered in the fifteen minutes or so since the slide: where was Furbar in all this trouble?

Little Furbar had gone on ahead of us down the route and we had to make sure he was safe. We bid our goodbyes to Jasminka and the villagers of Thado Koshigoan and hurried off to find our faithful porter. We had only traveled a few minutes farther down the path when we saw the total scale of damage done to the trail. Like a massive lava flow, all the debris had crashed away parts of the trail in several spots.

One steep section had been completely wiped clean for about sixty feet across and there on the other side sat Furbar, filthy and bleeding down his arm, but smiling as always and obviously glad we too were still in one piece. It took Hansah and me about twenty minutes to navigate up and around that portion of the slide to rejoin our companion and continue on toward the Lukla plateau. Still shaking from the experience, he had apparently walked past that finger of earth only seconds before it was wiped from existence. We cleaned and dressed his arm and though we were all still a little shaken, we walked on for the next few kilometers, joking together and pleased we'd survived the morning's affair.

~

We arrived at Furbar's place in Lukla dusty and drawn. His family had come out to greet us and they were obviously relieved. Word had already spread down the trail that some people may have been caught in the slide. Furbar's mother was first to see us plopping down the trail. She gasped and placed her hand over her heart, softly weeping as she held him tightly in her arms. His father talked the whole march back, holding Furbar's arm in his own and lamenting to the rest of us about the volatility of the mountain slopes.

He ushered us into their lodge and *up* to our rooms, already secured for the night. Of course, they resembled the other small quarters I had frequented throughout the trip. But I was grateful for my 7 x 9-foot hovel. It sported two beds (which I slammed together), a blanket for each, both of which I used for myself, a small night stand, and a bathroom down the hall for everyone on the second floor. *(Damn it,* I noticed, *we were in another two-story flat).*

The alternative, had it turned out to be a tragedy, was having my shredded corpse dug out from under a pile of mountainous rubble and shipped home without welcome or fanfare. I'd be dead and that would be that. Compared to a burial in rocks, I'd take a chilly room and a cold shower any day. It was even a blessing to breathe again, I thought as I valued the lower altitudes growing more prevalent toward the end of our trip. Reveling in the experience at hand was a concept I exploited as often as I could.

Like a typical youth, Furbar had already ventured off to

brag about his ordeal with his friends. Furbar's father ran the flight scheduling office for Lukla and was trying to book us onto an earlier flight for the following day. Though I was tired and spent, I actually looked forward to the conviviality that was sure to be part of that night in their lodge.

Nothing was certain for *Team Shizen* with regard to the weather anymore. The planes had stopped ferrying trekkers from Kathmandu early that morning because of fog, treacherous winds, and low-moving clouds. At present, it was 3:40 in the afternoon and just starting to clear on the mountain plateau. With a growing backlog of returning trekkers, I assumed that innumerable delays would stall my own return flight until around 9:00 a.m. the following day, if ever! This would override a mountain scenic tourist flight I had scheduled out of the Tribhuvan airstrip at 6:30 that morning as well. The landslide had delayed us by a couple of hours on our hike back to Lukla, and the clouds snuffed out any chance of us leaving when we wanted - *or so we thought.* Even if the visibility up there was as clear as a bell, the daylight was running out and we were being jammed against the coming night.

After our respective showers and we cleaned up our gear, Hansah and I strolled through the shops above the airstrip along an uneven cobblestone alley. As he had mentioned before, I was blessed with the gift of luck. I got rooms when others could not. I got to see Mount Everest through banks of trees and rolling clouds on every try when others spent thousands of dollars and days of their precious time trying to do the same. Today was no exception; the earth and fog had parted for me in ways that seemed more magical than chance. And though the day had been as full as any I'd had up there so far, it wasn't over yet.

I was the first to hear the distinct drone of the approaching aircraft. "Oh oh!" I blurted to Hansah as I held up my hands to the sound. I looked over at him with wide eyes and a smile; *I hear something, little buddy.* And in the next instant sure enough, the Dornier's reverse-engine thrust echoed through Lukla on the short uphill strip.

Suddenly people started pouring out of the sleepy alley shops and were heading for their gear, vacating their rooms, and charging toward the terminal. The afternoon weather had cracked through the clouds and the air services were running flights up and back again from Kathmandu. They hoped to drop in as many loads as they could and take others back before dark. *Business is business.* Hansah and I quickly predicted that we might get a ride home after all!

We hustled back to Furbar's family lodge and got with his dad for a new schedule. Furbar had since returned from his visit with friends and I thanked him for his help and friendship. Then I gave him a crisp $100 bill - twice the tip a regular porter gets for five days work. Their pay from the tour contractor is about $10 per day. Some packs are two to three times as heavy as mine, which, in my case, totaled about thirty pounds. Furbar got off easy with me and I'm sure I spoiled him rotten with his featherweight loads and our good natured company. Indeed, I think he'll be cursing me out for that with every new overbearing and troublesome client he gets.

As fate would have it, Hansah and I were told to gather our belongings and head to the departure terminal, just in case. The scheduling agent spit out our tickets and Furbar's dad personally walked us through security, baggage manifest stations, and into the passenger holding area like we were royal visitors. Once there, we waited with only ten others as the loads now were thinning out.

But, we did in fact wait. We waited, and waited. No more planes were coming in. Nothing could be heard to indicate a distant, familiar turboprop cracking off the Lukla valley walls. After the initial flurry of trekkers had plopped into the field that late afternoon, the clouds were coming down again, locking the field into a potentially foggy version of green-pea soup.

Though unsure that our luck was still knocking at the door, the cloud bank was holding against the mountain shelf about 300 feet above the airstrip. That's where the last of the upper slope had disappeared, as well as the hopes of us few remaining passengers. Most of us were quiet, not wanting by some karmic jinx to say something and spoil the chance that a last, daring aircraft may sneak its way in. From my own barnstorming exploits as a pilot and swooping dirt strips in farm fields to rescue lone skydivers from long walks home, I knew if a pilot was up there that had any gumption whatsoever, we still had a chance to get out. The minutes clicked by in silence, like a total eternity had surrounded the terminal area and suspended it in time.

By surprise, the passenger service agent ran in from the outside ramp and yelled into the room, "Number five!" We collectively looked around like, does that mean something to us? His thought was analogous to our own, *Hell yes that means you guys!* "Number five, let's go!" and he motioned us up with his hands - *Get the hell out of there!*

As one single spirit, we breathed a sigh of relief and started groping for our packs and jackets and stuffed souvenir bags. We scurried out to the passenger ramp and yes, I could see the distinct shape and blinking inbound lights of the approaching aircraft sliding up between the green valley peaks.

Much like the efficiency of a world-class drop zone, people jumped out of the plane during the engine-running offload and ran for cover. We clamored in on their heels, throwing our bags in the cargo hold and scrambling aboard for a seat. Again, in less than four minutes flat, the able flight crew had transitioned 30-plus passengers, all their luggage and manifest paperwork, and had taken off again in a swirl of outstanding air operations management.

I couldn't stop smiling as we lunged off the cliff-side edge of the short field runway and lifted off into the heights.

~

Our landing at Kat' was mixed with a beautiful lowland sunset and a rust-colored, smoggy haze from the dust and exhaust of thousands of cars in rush-hour traffic. Though spread out all over the hills and into the sprawling plains of the developing countryside, the city was still too small to hold its million-plus people. That afternoon, the airport-to-hotel journey found us wedged into another gridlock of musty, unkempt vehicles.

Between a horse-drawn potato cart vying for the median, and a listing, overcrowded bus at the curb with people hanging out the windows and clinging to the luggage racks, we were stopped for a string of Indian elephants walking trunk-to-tail across the street in front of our cars in the intersection ahead. They were herded along by a little guy with a stick wearing a soiled, button down shirt, dirty khaki shorts, and a pair of green, tattered zorries too small for his feet. Whatever these elephants were doing in this part of the city, I couldn't say. Who knew where they came from or where they were going after they passed. Once our car had moved up ahead, I couldn't see them anywhere. They had simply disappeared.

That night, I settled back into my refuge at the Tibet Guest House, and it didn't take me long to get out and roam the one-lane store-fronts to find yet another Korean restaurant. Once again I selected the *tol-sot bebimbop*. It was my night's *safest*, recurring meal. I could trust it; I liked the familiar taste of the vegetables and beef cooked and delivered in its own oven-hot stone serving pot. When I mixed it together with the sides of sweet yellow turnips, soy nuts glazed in a brown syrupy sauce, carrots, sprouts, and rice with red cayenne chili paste, it all went down like honey. I used to eat this meal habitually when I lived in Korea and it never ceased to satisfy me elsewhere on the planet.

Strolling through the Nepalese alleys in the darkened, often candle-lit shadows, I was reminded of a life I left far behind while stationed north of Seoul in Uijongbu, the little East Asian village was famous for its military camp life by day, and the ribaldry of its village night life after the sun went down. Thinking back on those spirited days, life was always filled with the international flare of bounding on assignment between Korea, Japan, Thailand, and the Philippines. Being a part of eligible twenty-year-olds from America, we always flirted with the girls in the bars. What resulted from the harmless fun in that sometimes got us married, divorced, or in trouble with the local MP's for making mischief they couldn't ignore.

But that was then, and this was now. Nepali nightclubs began to vibrate with the age-old sentiments as western tourists melted into their neon promises of cozy companionship and even better drinks. But at such a late hour, life was winding down in Nepal's crowded alley streets; shops were bringing down their aluminum sliding doors, closing to lock up for the night. Street merchants who had bested the greater portion of their day pushing silky garments, wooden artifacts, and brass souvenirs were beginning to slow down as well. The more prominent shop-keepers stayed open a bit longer to squeeze in one last sale before heading for home.

Colorful Thangka artwork, Durbar Square. Photo: B.T. Dormire

I strolled into a beautiful gallery of art and calligraphy just to look around. There were works in there so detailed that some of the originals took as long as two years of an artist's time to finish. Naturally, I wanted to buy everything in sight. Banally I resisted. How could I carry a large, ornately-framed oil painting of a Hindu God or a Sherpa and yak train against an Everest backdrop all over Kathmandu? *If I ever come back to Nepal,* I thought, which someday might be the case, I could always return this way and buy something for sure. Right, I promised myself again – *next time.* Stepping from store to store, I often convinced myself I'd return for a valuable keepsake. But in the same notion I knew it was a feat I always. . . *never accomplished.* There's always something busier to do on a trip, more important to discover than covering old ground.

The Nepalese have a universal saying. "Come into the store, looking is free. *So is our shipping.*" I liked what they had in there, each piece valued more highly depending on the talent of the artist and the duration of the work. I should have picked something up.

The night eventually took on a quiet, romantic feel to me, comfortable in its leisure and ambiance. I took a slow bicycle-rickshaw back to the hotel with nothing but crickets and the hushed whispers of lovers deciding what haughty mischief they could get into next. Spirits searching the darkness seemed to me the only semblance of life. I drifted past tiny, candlelit shrines and dwindling electrical bulbs, arcing frantically to supply their last bit of service for the night.

As I clung to the moods of the settling darkness, my gaunt chauffeur steered me down a maze of eerie, back ally haunts. I half-glanced at the shadows in this cranny or that, unaccustomed to being startled by anything in the night. But for some reason being alone in this element spooked me. I balked from what I perceived as hidden, masked images of ancient demons, growling at me from blackened piles of untended trash. And I shied from broken, rusted wrought-iron fence gates snarling at me in twisted, grotesque shapes. Coal-oil lamps lit the skeletal figures of the poor and crippled, huddled and crouched into dark, filthy corners and staring at me with soulless eyes. A few more turns of this and I was really going to start wondering if I wasn't headed to a stick-up, or an angry, Maoist bludgeoning. But at last, we turned back onto a main thoroughfare and eventually found the hotel.

Sitting back in the brick-lined patio garden under my room, I was immersed in the thoughts of what this day had been for me. For the most part, I never shied from walking the trails, alleys, or streets of Nepal in darkness or daylight; everyone was so helpful and friendly. Though the street merchants sometimes got a little pushy, I knew they were just trying to make a buck. Maybe they were working to pay for their dinner, or living day to day to support their families. Maybe they hustled to sell beaded jewelry or necklaces of ornamented Hindu symbols to earn penance for a challenging Karma. Some sold purses or scarves; some tried to demonstrate a flute or handmade, teakwood violin - miniature in size - but melodic and mystifying in its play just the same.

"Looking is free," they kept saying, so was their spunk. If you gave either their eyes or their merchandise a second glance, they had you. They'd chase after you with relentless determination. Unless you could divert them to another westerner, or just get rude and send them packing, they'd stay on you until you fled the market, screaming in terror.

And forget about giving a kid a rupee or two to shut them up. I did this once in Durbar Square and even looked around to see that we weren't being watched or followed by a throng of other little deviants. "Okay kid, you're cute and you handed me a good story – so here's fifty cents, now get lost."

Well, that was nothing less than the biggest mistake I ever made. Twenty kids flew in from out of nowhere and swarmed down on me like locusts, and more kids were running over to join in the frenzy. I finally had to get my guide to gently shoo them away. But even then, some of the younger, fearless ones clung to me like remora sucker-fish do to a symbiont shark. The children laughed and tugged at my pockets and I finally took about three dollars' worth of paper rupees and coins and threw them into the afternoon wind.

I pulled open my empty pockets and threw up my hands in surrender. It was wonderful to watch them scurry off happy, wealthy, and squealing.

Day Six was at an end, yet there were still places to tour in Kathmandu and I'd be hitting them tomorrow. As I settled inside my warm hotel covers for the night, I was sore from dodging rock slides and skirting treacherous paths, and my joints ached despite the glucosamine I had sent to me from the States. Preparing for the uphill climbs and downhill poundings was prudent, no doubt. But the mountain; *these mountains,* as I would soon discover, always won out in the end. My longing to fulfill this Nepali trek had certainly hit its mark. I reviewed what I'd learned on the trail, high above the crux of the civilization I knew back in the world. All I could do was acknowledge what I've probably justified a thousand times before, under a thousand different demands:

That I did what I set out to do, and I've never been so satisfied in my life.

❦

What Is Learned and What Remains.

Day 7 - October 13, 2012

I thought being on vacation meant lying in bed with the love of your life stretched out in a euphoric bliss until room service arrived with breakfast. Because I was on my own at night in the farthest reaches of Nepal, the only options I had to compare to this were going to bed by myself and pulling a granola bar off the nightstand in the morning (my personal exemplification of room service). I had little or no idea what being pampered was all about over here. My pattern of hitting the sheets in the still of night and not getting enough rack before the next adventure began was an ongoing routine. Once again, Ram Hari from *Shizen Treks* had arranged for a day guide and he got to the hotel not long after my 5 a.m. alarm. Before I knew it, I was piling into a microscopic Fiat and we were on another harrowing ride to the Tribhuvan Domestic Air Terminal.

We got out of Lukla the previous afternoon under the graces of good timing and a reprieve in the weather. Because of that, and if we didn't crash the car on the trip over, I was going to make it to the airport cattle-call and not miss my scenic mountain flight, set to launch at 6:45 a.m. As usual, Hansah was there to facilitate my transfer around the hundred or so trekkers standing in the outside lines waiting to get through security. He walked me past the baggage scanners right up to the Yeti Airways ticket agent and I checked in without delay.

After a quick passport scan, I was off to the inside holding area and that's where I told Hansah goodbye. I had given him a well-earned $200 tip for our five days on the mountain and another $30 in remaining pocket change before we parted that morning. He'd been a standing guardian and a friend to me throughout the journey and kept me out of plenty of trouble. I never got shoved off the valley-side of the trails by the jube-ques. He pulled me from the debris of a rock slide which almost ended everything in disaster. And probably the most important, he kept me on my toes with Kate and the other female groups from the Three Sisters Treks.

Yeti's twin-engine British Aerospace Jetstream 41, the Everest Express, took off inside golden rays of the morning sun streaking through clouds of smoke and smog. We had made it up over the city to begin our flight along the great Himalayan range. Skirting the vast aerial landscape and from the moment we reached our best viewing altitude, I could see beyond Nepal's border and well into China's claim on Tibet. The flight was basically an out-and-back which began by speeding straight into the brilliant sunrise. Being plopped in a far-side seat with nothing but people's heads and a relentless glare to look at on the outbound leg, I couldn't see one damn thing.

Banking for the inbound leg, the plane's trajectory eventually turned us toward the peaks and gave my side of the fuselage a much better look at the mountains on our return. The young stewardess ushered passengers to the cockpit one at a time for observations from the pilot's perspective. My turn came as we angled in on the Lhotse peaks which were adjacent to Mount Everest itself. I gathered by the pitch of the aircraft that my initial concerns about a lousy experience were going to be relieved as I watched the great summits come into focus away from the glare of the sun.

The initial views on climb-out were something out of a

pictured storybook. We passed lush, green hillsides in the Kodari Valley with its perfectly terraced slopes. These arced into little ravines that eventually made way for the river canyons and steep forests that painted the growing castle-like mountains as we slowly rose in height. Then, the great peaks began to come into view: Pangma, Numbar, Cho-Oyu, Nuptse, Everest, Lhotse, Chamlang, and Makalu. Not all of these were 8,000 meters, but their immutable reputations for being the toughest climbs on earth left nothing to chance for the dreamer and expert alike.

As always, I would have opted to fly right on top of the peaks to take unparalleled photos I could brag about back home. Getting close enough, however, to satisfy my personal whims was not about to happen. People in the plane would have lost their kittens or screamed bloody murder in panic as I'd have the pilots diving and slipping through the jagged narrows to see if I could spot any climbers on an ascent. No, there were too many variables with mountain weather, international litigation beyond anyone's imagination, and probably prison sentences up the yazoo for penetrating Nepal's airspace anywhere near the sacred Sagarmatha National Park (*the name for Everest on Nepal's side of the border*).

Throughout my trek, I had tried to get a chopper flight up into the interior and over the base camp valley, figuring that would get me the proximity I'd need for an adequate thrill. This proved futile only because it would have been exorbitant in price to do so alone - more than $2,400 for a quick pass around Everest's walls of rock and ice. I got one helicopter fare as low as $1,800 and if I could find two other people to go; we could split the fee and get a great look at the massive mountain perch. No takers though; so there would be no personal helicopter ride for me on this vacation.

Besides, I think by hiking into the realms of the vast Himalayan expanse, a person gets a better appreciation for the mental and physical efforts of getting there. By climbing, say, the 18,000-foot Kala Patthar for a look at territory few humans will ever see, a higher value is set on the afterglow of the experience.

What was better, I wondered, a twenty-minute helicopter flight, or ten-day mountain trek? One option is a lot lazier than the other and may be just as fleeting in memory a few years down the road. The climb, however, imprints itself onto one's psyche for the rest of their life. That's the difference between the two.

Maybe that's why I feel the need to come back to Nepal and execute a much longer hike. My first adventure was the five-day Everest Short Tour, (similar, as they say, to packing ten-pounds of poop in a two-pound bag). So, a Base Camp trek of seventeen days or more would be a much more impressive and appreciated endeavor.

Acclimating and going slow are the keys to success with any high-altitude hike. I heard two British hikers had died in their sleep during the week I was there, no one mentioned why. Authorities later believed as I first thought as well, that it might be a compounded instance of HACE on the one hand, and carbon monoxide poisoning from an ill-heated room on the other. Rushing up to Gorak Shep, which was 5,100 meters and the last lodging outpost prior to climbing the Kala Patthar - Everest's best overlook, might have done them in. Who really knew for sure?

~

The minute I returned from Yeti Airway's scenic flight, I was presented with none other than - you guessed it - an additional silk prayer scarf to add to my growing collection. For a little something extra on this trip we also received an 8 x 10 aviation flight certificate handed out by the lovely Nepali stewardess. She was every inch of five-feet tall and the spitting image of a Nepalese Harley pin-up girl. She was buxom, wore a short navy-blue skirt and a red blouse tied off just above her navel, and had a dark, cool looking airline cap with something that resembled a red feather in it. I thought to myself, *Namaste Indeed!*

After the flight's three-point landing and taxiing all over the runway, it was still pretty early at the airport - 8:25 a.m. by my watch. My driver was patiently waiting for me outside the terminal grounds and he shared a few cross words with other drivers stalled out or blocking the way of our car. It was a ruse, I suspected, to get me to drive off with them if I wasn't previously satisfied or already committed to a tour.

I was pretty busy myself, getting a persistent street vendor to stop trying to sell me live snakes through the vehicle's right side window. Even with all our distractions, my guide and I gingerly maneuvered out of the airport parking fiasco and into the charm of Kathmandu's morning traffic commute.

What a blooming nightmare!

After being sideswiped by a rusty passenger bus, and running a bicycle-rickshaw off into a ditch near the golf course outside the airport - (Fore!), we pretty much had the rest of the day to ourselves. It was time to set off for the first stop on our remaining, whirlwind city agenda.

Bhaktapur was the ancient, well-preserved kingdom district with its host of honored holy men to greet us at every shrine. It bolstered a venerated, 700-year-old architecture of wood and stone, and had all the usual merchants and beggars as well. Once again, the cripples on the outskirts of these tourist draws gnawed at me the worst. Young or old, they were always there. Some used pieces of old tire tread on their hands to drag themselves along, sliding on their bottoms on a skid plate of rubber or plastic, sometimes corrugated aluminum siding, sometimes nothing at all.

Many beggars held out a hand for food or rupees. I had read in the book, *Siddhartha*, by Hermann Hesse that the act of begging by certain ascetic holy men was their way of life. That by abolishing worldly possessions and desires, they could focus more closely on the spiritual gains of ascension and seek their inner divinity and esoteric beliefs. They only needed a little sustenance to get by each day and the blessings toward the unity of life could begin.

One little boy walked beside me for some time through Bhaktapur's brick-paved alleys without saying a word. Then finally he said, "Please sir, I don't want any money, just buy me a book. My school says I can join them if I bring my own book." Now that was something I could relate to, so I did. We slid into the bookstore he pointed out and he bee-lined straight to a dictionary of English and Nepalese phraseology. It was almost as big as he was and it was a quick ten bucks. Things seemed just a little too familiar between him and the store manager, like they'd done this bit a thousand times a day. After the transaction, I assumed I was being taken for a ride, but the singular effort he made to get me to acquiesce was well worth the price of admission.

Bhaktapur Bell Shrine & Traditional Pagoda. Photo: B.T. Dormire

The ancient city itself boasted the greatest concentration of temples in one place for all of Nepal. There were temples for the gods of power, luck, prosperity, long life, fertility and virility, honor and truth. Many shrines were dedicated to fighting off demons, and those were adorned with carvings or statues of cobras and lions, as well as many more shapes depicting warriors bracing for battle.

Everywhere throughout Nepal's temples and touristy

venues, there were these pick-up guides who swooped in to usurp the historical tutelage away from the regular escort, paid for or not. They would just come up and start talking about the rich details of architecture or the perennial significance of an honored place - and they'd do it because they could. Their spiel was down to the letter. In Bhaktapur the guide who attached himself to us latched on from the second we got out of the car, but the driver didn't do much to discourage him from leaving, so on he went about the royal heritage of the site we were about to enter.

I had breakfast in the Natalya Square Teahouse, an ancient 600-year-old temple turned into a chai and biscuit café. The wood carved lattices and eaves overhung the balconies near our table on the second floor above the big town square. Across the yard there were people giving their morning devotionals and marking the red, chalky tikka powder on their foreheads. Once again, this was to acknowledge that they had prayed and given thanks for the day. They also put flower petals in their hair and walked on about their business. Some placed colored rice grains on their foreheads instead. It was all very ritualistic. From my breakfast overlook, I could see the surrounding temples and a raised cement stage-like slab that was busy with merchants, school marms, and religious tenants practicing prayers to the sky and no one else in particular.

A unit of city police was forming up on the slab for the start of their day; their rendition of a stateside guardmount I suppose. It consisted of three constables on bicycles, and four or five others on foot. Swirling in and around the cops and their formation, and spilling over to the worshipers touching the shrine for their prayers, there was a group of small kids playing a game called *tuggie*. Right there on the raised stone platform, the children threw around a sort of hairy hacky-sack at each other. It was similar to tag only you had to nail everybody in sight with this tough little beanbag ball to stay in the game. The kid with the *tuggie* got to throw at all the others running around inside the imaginary boundary. As long he or she kept hitting them with each toss, this removed them from the game, and the slaughter continued. If the hacky-sack missed a target altogether, then it was a free-for-all to whoever snatched it up and chucked it at somebody else.

One little girl in particular couldn't miss. She was wearing a small cotton dress, dark - or dirty, I couldn't tell which from the balcony restaurant. Her black, silken hair was tied back in a ponytail and she had an arm and aim that any little league coach would die for. She was about ten or eleven and the other kids stayed clear of her while she was "It." Another girl threw wild shots that wound up hitting the cops (and making them laugh - they must have played when they were kids too). Some old lady sitting on a shop step and pealing chestnuts received the flying hacky in her lap. She drew it from the cradle of her sari and threw it back in the game like an old pro. It was a very personal moment in the life of these villagers and I was glad to have witnessed it over my cheese omelet, toast, and fruit-flavored jam.

I walked through many of the site's alleyways and fended off dozens of beggar kids. But eventually I wound up over in pottery square. This was where they cured handmade clay pots in straw-fed kilns. They fired these pots in ingenious mud-ovens covered in bales of straw to insulate the curing from the inside - out. Pots, tea-kettles, and vases of all shapes and sizes 'cooked' on separate racks from the heat of natural sources for at least four days, and then they were shuttled into an artist's studio where young, obscure painters made masterpieces in pottery art drawings. A lot of the black painted images reminded me of the symmetry in the Ta moko Maori tribal facial tattoos of Tahiti and the Polynesian Isles.

As we left Bhaktapur, a thought kept running through my mind like a song:

God's gift to man is his spirit. Man's gift to earth is his talent. What is unveiled from ages of our creativity, rises from the insights of the poor.

The next site we encountered was in the heart of the city at a place called, Pashupatinath. Its golden pagoda roofs and several temple shrines were easily distinguish above the city skylights and depicted the Hindu's most sacred spiritual grounds - a ritual crematory for families from all over the provinces surrounding Kathmandu.

There was an interesting comment made by the pick-up guide we inherited outside the crematory. He said, "When tourists travel to different shrines in the city, it must be the same as seeing different countries as well. We are always learning something from the people we visit, and they are learning something from us."

I had to agree.

Furthermore, he knew every nuance of the family rituals of cleansing and blessing a body for cremation. "The pyres are busy day and night," he said. "They collapse in on themselves burning into a pile on the stone slabs overlooking the river." The whole visit was an immeasurable lesson that I couldn't have gotten without him.

Thinking about what that Nepali guide had said, I looked around at the spectacle of the families honoring their departed. There were bathing rituals performed by one family for their beloved deceased, washing the feet and face of the body to prepare its way for the next life to come. Another family was further down the river spreading the ashes of their cremated relative in the water so it flowed with the spirits to nirvana.

There were monkeys all over these grounds with holy men dressed in all sorts of ceremonial costumes and headdress to take on the role of the different gods to bless tourists like me. I was pictured with the Monkey God, Hanuman, who symbolized all the inspiration one needs to face and conquer any ordeal. Often referred to as one of the most popular idols in Hindu beliefs, he teaches the unlimited power of devotion that lies unused in each of us. Venerated as the undefeated fighter of demons, the blessing of Hanuman gives ardent devotees the greatest faith in the most troubling times.

Blessing of the Monkey God, Hanuman, for strength & perseverance.

Photo by Hansah.

I thought about what our barefoot, enterprising friend had said in the beginning footfalls or our stop at Pashupatinath. We indeed learn a lot about the diversity of people and places when we go somewhere new. We get a feel for how they live and what they eat. We soak up the character and culture of a place, even though, as in my case, we may only skirt the surface of discovering what it's all about. So in turn, the people of these lands learn from us as well. They always asked me where I was from. Not necessarily because they were nosy, but more likely to keep their curiosity going and maybe win me over as their new, important friend.

Anyone from America's direction is going to be of interest to locals because they always want to know who we are and what we do. If we only profess to be from a general location in the states, "I'm from the West," then they tie that reluctance or caution in our demeanor to the overall character of our country. A more outwardly disposition comes forth as we open up to people instead. "I'm from

Colorado. We have a lot of mountains there too."

I gathered that Americans overall - once they were warmed up or charmed - were more approachable than, say, the standoffish Europeans or the more secular Asians, like the Koreans or Chinese. These individuals are especially unique in that regard. They stick to their own - like glue - and rarely venture anywhere to extremes, especially without a reason to share or explore someplace new and provocative. But if you say hello to them in their own language, they light up like the sun and pull you into their midst.

I liked watching the Japanese trekkers who were definitely more independent behind their cultural privacy. Once I broke the ice, however, they were the friendliest people I encountered out there, really enjoying my salutations and authentic Japanese greetings when I passed them on the trail. Surprised that I could recognize them at a glance, I could tell the difference between their rich, thematic greetings, the hearty Koreans with their almost bashful acknowledgment that I'd said hello, and the determined Chinese who looked as if I'd dissected their plans to take over the world.

There's a refined confidence to the Japanese that's sublimely amazing to experience. Wherever I saw them on the mountain, they had what resembled an American self-assurance that surrounded their entire, unassuming persona. It seemed to me that they were borne of a people who once tried ruling the entire Asian continent, who walked humbly assured that they could do it again if they felt like it, anytime they wanted.

~

So, what have I gained from my extravagance? That I enjoy traveling? That my convivial attempts to socialize with strangers in foreign countries qualifies me to discuss personal confidences in lectures or public forums? Do my personal observations transcend the casual wayfaring I do through distant countrysides when people rely on me to learn from such experience? Should I even pretend to inspire others on the nuances of visiting exotic lands when, more often than not, they may never be able to go there themselves? I think *'Yes'* to all of these points, if for nothing else but to look outside a hometown window and wonder what treasures wait for us beyond our own front door.

We are all enlightened by experience, drawn to the smiles of others who accomplish similar, spectacular events. And of those who stroll by us in an airport concourse? They too can leave us spellbound, tricked by romantic afterthoughts. Can we survive our emotions while remembering the glances of a prospective heartthrob? Is there someone close to us right now, just aching for that first 'Hello'? Will we ever see them again if we don't take that timely, initial chance? I'll often ponder a girl who caught my eye; wondering if she would also walk with me in awe through ancient river gorges or extravagant hotel lobbies?

As always, my frivolous conjecture frequently blends with other's down-to-earth reality, and I drift past them unnoticed. People go about their busy lives pretending *not* to think the same, and I stay mellowed in my own, personal indulgence.

In traveling the world by myself, there is no surprise then, that by reaching the splendor of this melodious Nepal, true life is reflected back at me in return – Namaste.

If I could improve myself more for the people I've met in my travels, I certainly would. I'd learn a few extra lines of their native tongue or enjoy some of their traditional cuisine. But I'm lazy and suffer from an inherent lack of courage to do something new – *most of the time.* Trekking the Himalayas will always be intriguing to me. It was ten-fold the experience I thought I'd ever receive.

If I had any regrets on the trip, it might play into wishing I could have taken better pictures of the indigenous people in their natural surroundings; worshiping at their favorite shrines, or talking more to outgoing monks at the giant stupas. I'd have asked a new girl I bumped into, Karen, for her number while we lumbered

B.T. Dormire

around the world heritage site at Bodhnath.

Maybe I'd have purchased a trinket more meaningful to my experience than the first offer shoved at me just to quiet a pushy, pretty vendor girl. When I bought her necklace of moonpearls, she pressed me into taking her entire remaining stock. I succeeded in avoiding a financial rout, but her beautiful smile was hard to resist.

My last full day in Kathmandu was a smooth, busy one, as were they all. I gained a perspective of Nepal's spiritual diversities that garnered a further respect for their culture, their faith, and their seemingly happy, pleasant way of life.

I discovered from hiking the fringe of the Himalayan mountains, that stronger trekkers conquer these heights as a leisure, a past time they thrive upon just for kicks. Still, the more harrowing adventurists carry a professional diligence about them. They endure getting themselves or their clients to the tops of these great peaks. And those who lose their heart to the people and landscape of Nepal do so from an outright obsession with its cultural preeminence and its geographic beauty. Other apparently resonant motives include Nepal's haunting religious diversity, and the promise that the country will stay the same as it's always been until they return.

I've only just begun to dabble in Himalayan potential, but as I've seen from this trip alone, I will be getting back into its clutches with a passion. Nepal's mountains can be twice as high as any stateside peak, and its rivers run wild from ice-aged glaciers. The technical aspects of crevasse travel and mountain rescue, or the thousand-foot vertical ice climbs that lure younger, healthier crowds play bigger roles in expeditions than I will ever challenge. However, trekking to 18,000-foot overlooks or through summit passes rich in history and adventure, might be better suited for me in the end. I'll have to wait and see if the smoke of a village cooking fire lures me back to its grace instead.

~

The morning of Day 8 was like any other on this journey -

a crazy, unconscionable drive through the fading darkness of Kathmandu. We bounced over sidewalks, swerved wildly around frightened pedestrians, and charged through its early morning streets; and that was just to find the coffee shop. It had me wishing I could sleep it off for the next twenty hours straight in some high mountain cottage with a beautiful brunette. But I couldn't do that just yet. I still had to catch this one final flight off the *Roof of the World* and I wasn't about to miss it.

Onward ho, Driver, Pilot, and Spiritual Compass!

I sat in the passenger holding area of the Tribhuvan international terminal and watched the new sunrise glimmering in from the east. It seemed to compliment a mood I had paralleled waking up and recalling the splendor of the trek I'd just accomplished. I remembered the spiritual significance I felt peering off a towering ledge toward the Drengka Monastery nestled at the base of the 19,500-foot Khumbila Peak. Locals called it the Holy Mountain; I admired its mammoth scale from the Syangboche plateau. I thought about the effort it would take to get back to Nepal. I thought about getting better at resumes for the journeyman-materializations I'd need to survive moving from one employer to the next. To live in the lavishness of a permanent vacation, I needed a job!

And..., I thought about Kate.

I wondered if she'd been affected by the earthquake while staying in Namche Bazar. It was just up the hill from my own little dirt-dive and I knew they got hit between the eyes with that 5-pointer-plus. Jolts like that one are felt for miles. I wrote her from the Tibet Guest House Wi-Fi on my last night in Nepal, but I waited for days after that with no word in return. I assumed she was still on her climb, though I also wondered if she'd ever answer the emails I sent. I mentioned the exploits we talked about at the restaurant; about the rock slide I dodged hoping she wasn't in one of her own. I talked openly with her through my mails, expressed life in colorful anecdotes to send her assurances that I was still in her court.

The more time that elapsed between us, the more I realized that if she didn't write soon, maybe she wouldn't. If she wanted to make a connection, she could easily write me back and I'd respond. If I never heard from her again, not even a peep, it would be my own little disappointment and nothing else. I'd learn to accept it.

I wondered if someday out of the blue I'd receive her Australian-based email. Would I realize who it was, would I be free or affluent enough at the time to respond? A thought crossed my mind that maybe she *really was the heiress* to her family's mineral mining empire; something she crowed to me about after our third rum - and, as I thought about it - to test me for a reaction. I acknowledged her lighthearted comment with only, *"Wow, I could dig that."*

I imagined Kate being every woman to me, someone I'd never have to look away from to compare to another. We wore those silly party hats and even in jest, I'd wanted laughs like that with a woman for a while. When I was roaming Europe as a student a million years ago, was she the girl I'd brushed into on the Eiffel Tower and asked for a picture? Or did we flirt in the squares of old Amsterdam after dark and not even know who we were? If I asked her, would she stroll with me and hang off my arm at sunset on a Costa Rican beach? In the long run, could her beauty and spirit stand up to my whims for frivolity or adventure? I knew one thing for certain, that without any contact between us whatsoever we'd never know if love would prevail.

Had Nepal taught me something else up there? Was I thinking not just about Kate, but of every woman I ever loved or cared for? Could I still mean as much to a woman as I wanted to feel from Kate? Was I wrong in never saying so to them? *"Darling, I love you."* Or more wrong in saying it too much?

As the Gulf Air jetliner streaked away from Heaven's own legion of thrones, I nestled into my seat and curled up under the tissue they called an airline blanket. The hectic state of my journey to and from the Himalayas, and the city tours that hurled me from one end of Kathmandu to the other, certainly kept me wishing that I never had to leave. I knew, however, that no matter where I wound up again in the world, I would always be hooked on the romance and friendship I found *Dallying in Nepal.*

❧

Web References, Equipment,

And Further Readings

The websites and books noted below helped me connect with the best trekking services and information I could find. They inspired me to begin a longstanding affection for everything tied to climbing, hiking, and trekking. I discovered new interests on mountains, expanded my education and eco-sensitivity. I grew in self-assurance from technical and academic training, improved my physical fitness, set higher goals for myself and achieved them without the slightest pause. Throughout my travels I have seen adventure, persistence, philosophy, determination, suffering, gratitude, camaraderie, awe, respect, and even love. From all that I have mentioned above, everything suited my needs for tackling the Short Everest Tour I accomplished in October 2012.

There are many levels of trekking adventure that one can pursue based on their particular talents, degree of fitness, and ultimate desire. From walking around a neighborhood lake, or topping a great summit, the challenge is up to each of us to get up and go.

To be fully ordained in mountaineering at high altitude extremes, I read several volumes of how-to books and the best of mountain literature for a refinement of techniques, motivation, and intrigue. The books listed herein are just a fraction of those I read which moved me past the confines of a cluttered living room, an empty television lineup, and a wish instead, that I'd gone someplace important at least once in my life. I hope as well, that you find the inspiration you require to get out and reward yourself with a trip through Nature's brilliant expanse.

Byron Dormire

Essential Websites

Nepal Trekking Tours - Shizen Treks P, Ltd.
www.nepaltrekkingtrips.com

3 Sisters Treks - Women's Trekking Service.
www.3sistersadventuretrek.com

Nepal Hiking Team - A complete solution to hiking Nepal.
www.nepalhikingteam.com

Mountain Madness - Scott Fischer. www.mountainmadness.com

Edmund Viesturs official Website. www.edviesturs.com

Great Outdoors - Inspiration and Information.
www.greatoutdoors.com

Best Mountaineering Literature. www.summitpost.org/best-mountaineering-literature

Climbing, Hiking, and Mountaineering. www.summitpost.org

Swayambhunath Hindu Monkey Temple http://tripideas.org/the-sacred-monkey-temple-kathmandu/

Equipment and Training Guidelines

In Nepal, food and creature comforts for my initial trek was not as imperative as one might need for a more serious expedition. Having traveled for multiple days on the trail, I was always within a few kilometers of a hot meal and a bath, cold or otherwise. Nevertheless, I took a large portion of Great Value Mountain Trail Mix which fit neatly into the side pouch on my pack. Snickers and Mars bars had a monopoly up in the Himalayan tea houses and I was glad they were so abundant at every stop. Water abounded in bottled form at every trail shelter, village hostel, and hamlet café. As climbs reached into the higher realms, or I wanted to fill my Nalgene from plentiful sources of boiled or mountain-fed snow melt, I preferred the compact and efficient pump-style Katadyn Water Microfilter found at most sporting goods outlets.

Clothing psychology remained intact from my past - *'loose and in layers'*. I used a thin pair of Under-Armor tops and bottoms, 511 shirts and pants for their loose and comfortable fit, and the ever-faithful smart wool socks of varying thickness depending on my altitude and difficulty of terrain. Boot types vary per person, and I worried a bit about fording streams or slogging up snow lines, neither of which proved significant on this particular venture being so low on the peaks. If however, I would have gone any higher I might have fared better with a solid waterproof hiking boot, or even plastics with crampons for the snow routes above 15,000 feet. The nice thing about how refined this industry is in Nepal, you can find nearly every authentic, name brand outfitter based in most of the larger villages, meeting every conceivable need for clothing and climbing apparel. Rent or purchase - you won't go without a trifle on a Nepalese trek.

Picking the right gear for the appropriate conditions, with tips, lessons, and advice on everything from cooking, crevasse rescue, to basic survival, I chose the compilation from Stephen Cox and Kris Fulsaas: *Mountaineering- Freedom of the Hills, 8th Edition.* It's definitely the climber's ultimate resource.

❧

Further Readings

Joe Bindloss, Bradley Mayhew: Lonely Planet Series - Trekking in Nepal

Stephen Cox and Kris Fulsaas: Mountaineering- Freedom of the Hills, 8th Edition

Jim Curran: K2 - The Story of the Savage Mountain

Tessa Feller, Culture Smart Series: Nepal - The Essential Guide to Customs and Culture

Hermann Hesse: Siddhartha, and, The Seasons of the Soul

Jon Krakauer: Into Thin Air

Charles Mercer: Rachel Cade

Henrietta Merrick: In the World's Attick

Reinhold Messner: All 14 Eight-Thousanders

Eric Newby: Great Ascents

Fiona Roberts: A Beard in Nepal

Edmund Viesturs: No Shortcuts to the Top, and, The Will to Climb

Stephen Venables: A Slender Thread

Aron Ralston: Between a Rock and a Hard Place

Best of luck to you and warm, safe travels.

~ Namaste! ~

☯